THE TALENT EMERGENCY

Dear Jen—
You are an amazing
inspiration to so many people.
So excited to be part of
your journey!
[signature]

THE

Team Engineering

TALENT

How to Attract Best Talent

EMERGENCY

Creating the Ultimate Culture for Your Company

NICOLE MARTIN

The Talent Emergency

Publisher:
Nicole Martin
HRBoost, LLC
www.hrboost.com
847-736-5085

Publishing Consultant:
Professional Woman Publishing
www.pwnbooks.com

ISBN: 978-0-578-18935-2

For my children, may you live with conscious presence that redefines being present.

CONTENTS

PREFACE

In 2017, if you are leading a business, a team, perhaps even your own career and you have not realized you are witnessing the greatest shift of human capital in our lifetime, then this book is for you. *The Talent Emergency* is intended to state exactly what we are on the brink of in the United States. The coming five years will bring a serious situation to the forefront and for many businesses in the middle market this may even come unexpectedly.

Any "emergency" can be dangerous and the inability to attract, retain, develop and/or source talent is indeed a dangerous reality to be facing, let alone reactively in business. Yet, for years, I have been serving businesses only to find they are not prepared. Many do not even truly understand the skills shortage. Imagine, a business running an advertisement for an opening for 280 days with the intent of seeking talent. At what point does the business realize the talent is not there? At what point do they consider something must happen proactively to address the gap?

What I once thought was common knowledge I have now discovered is not. This book will aim to demonstrate how every business must come up with a strategy to meet every employee on their journey to joy and purpose or risk losing their talent to the competition. In fact, the talent may in fact become the competition. Work is personal and businesses must begin integrating strategies to acknowledge this fact. Office is a verb in this decade while work ethic, values and motivations are not universal. Yet, businesses are still developing one size fits all policies and it seems numerous businesses are seemingly unaware of the threat of ending up without the best talent on their side. The talent has won and it will choose where it wants to be.

Unlike their large-company counterparts, the middle market can often lack the time and resources to build infrastructure and processes that are beyond core business objectives. Yet, every business must develop a competitive advantage in today's turbulent economy. This can only be done with people.

This is not a new phenomenon. Businesses have long competed for talent. However, for the first time businesses will be competing over a talent pool whereby there simply will not be enough talent to meet demand in our country. Not every business is sourcing globally. And, worst of all, the United States could continue to suffer in the global context.

Being an employer of choice was once a "nice to have" but suddenly it is a "must have." Why? Consider that 2/3 of Millennials aim to be entrepreneurs[1] and 50% of mid-career or seasoned executives are planning to exit the talent pool by the year 2020. If you work in the real world, and I know you do, three years is not very long. We are not discussing a simple change initiative; we are discussing a paradigm shift.

In this book, I will aim to present practical solutions and case studies of real businesses facing the paradigm shift. I will share real stories from businesses that have successfully built competitive advantage through their people. With my insights I hope to share the ways in which any business can begin to transform their approach to working through people. Businesses must overcome generational differences, build appreciation vs. recognition and invest in creating the value proposition that inspires the intrapreneur in everyone. Building bench strength for a sustainable future will require people to come together in a meaningful way in the workplace. This book is not just about business; this book is about people. *The Talent Emergency* will require every business to look at how they meet talent in a different way.

ACKNOWLEDGEMENTS

I thank God for the fortune of being granted the passion to pursue life affirming work. *The Talent Emergency* was something that was undeniable to me and must be communicated. It was a simple idea and something I presumed everyone must know of and yet day after day, I found person after person did not know. I became driven to share what I know but more importantly, offer solutions and hopefully inspire many to lead from wherever they are. We all deserve to find work that we enjoy and that serves the greater good. This has all grown into more than I expected and I am deeply grateful to those that have helped to make it happen.

Though writing a book can feel like a solitary initiative, I must thank Brian… for whom I am blessed. There are no words to express my gratitude for my beautiful husband who empowers me to be true to my calling. He has always supported my commitment to learning and education and his support to me as his equal partner in life has been everything.

I would like to thank all those who encouraged, inspired, supported and contributed to making this book a better tool to put into the hands of business leaders and practitioners. I owe a special debt of gratitude to the REAL STORY and REAL EMPLOYER OF CHOICE contributors that have brought effective concepts and practices to life for the reader. It is their first-hand experience and expertise and my privilege of knowing and/or working with them that encouraged me to ask them to submit their short story. It is my pleasure to feature them. They have all consented and I am very grateful for their willingness to contribute and for their leadership. (See their contributions at the end of every chapter and Chapter 8, "Strategies & Dividends from a Few of the Best!")

To our clients, who have partnered with our firm and implemented our recommendations only to witness with us the incredible positive results in working through people. Great leaders committed to creating high performance organizations. It has been such fun to work with you and support your visions in partnership to create workforce alignment.

To Linda Ellis Eastman and Sarah Victory, two beautiful women who provided support to me and truly embraced my vision. They have helped me grow this past year and their advice on many aspects of this overall project was pivotal.

To the HRBoost team, this book could not be a reality if it were not for all our Consultants in the field delivering our brand promise. We bring Joy and Purpose to people through their work but it begins with each of us. I would like to specifically express gratitude for the dedication of Suzan Quinn Mayworm and Mansi Patel. Without your attention to details and ensuring that each event, presentation, speech, and communication reflected our belief that presence is more than just being present, it would all be for not.

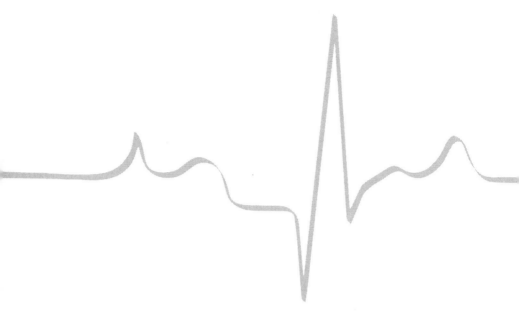

PART ONE

The Paradigm Shift

"A series of peaceful interludes punctuated by intellectually violent revolutions and in those revolutions one conceptual world view is replaced by another."

—THOMAS KUHN

CHAPTER ONE

The Looming Crisis to Business at Large

A crisis is often thought of as a particularly bad or critical state of affairs, arising from a number of negative and unpredictable factors. Typically, it would call for a difficult decision or change to be made. In the case of the *talent emergency*, many of the factors that are beginning to converge to reveal a looming crisis were in fact predicted. In some cases, each factor has in fact been studied at great length. Yet, seemingly, we are unprepared. Such a crisis, in this case, does not just happen, but rather it is driven by a number of external influences. Depending on your focus you may see only one or two elements of change in your day to day experience. In reality, all of the factors are right before us, looming already. If you are in business, you have less than five years before impacts are fully realized across industry, demographic and regions in the United States.

Changing Demographics

You may have heard about the "talent war" but in case you missed it...the talent has in fact won! The Bureau of Labor Statistics studies have released statistics reporting nearly 26 million workers will exit the talent pool by 2020. With skill shortages on the horizon, those that differentiate themselves as employers of choice will have a competitive advantage in attracting talent. However, even those employers will actively strive to retain the existing talent in the coming decade. The global competition will shape an intense environment where every business will be forced to develop programs to retain, attract and develop talent for the sustainable future. The emerging threat on sustainable business is most significant when reviewing apparent demographic shifts in the United States.

For the past century, the world experienced rapid growth. Historically, it took from 1800 to 1927 for the world to grow from one billion people to two billion people. Then, in the thirty three years that followed, the world grew to three billion in 1960. It only took fifteen years to reach four billion and then, in less time yet again, the world mushroomed to five billion in 1987. In the twelve years that followed, the world achieved six billion in 1999. Despite large adult populations in child bearing years, social trends in the last half of the twentieth century resulted in a dramatic decline in fertility rates as well as the transformation of the role of women in society.[2] Reportedly, world population passed the seven billion mark back in 2011. While these population trends globally have been rising for the past century, experts at the Institute of Demography and Futurists alike see a peak as early as 2040, followed by a strong downward decline with a global population as low as five billion by 2100. Thus, peak population is sooner than many realize. Despite global fertility rates, the United States in contrast (see Figure 1.1) will not experience an increase in population from its native population. Similarly, more developed regions will remain mostly unchanged as well. The unprecedented shifts in human capital pose a significant external influence to every business in a global context. Adding to the element of complexity are the profound implications on the available talent pool and more specifically, the age demographic within the talent pool in the coming years to 2020. The global developments mask considerable variations between countries and regions as a result of very different fertility, mortality and migration trends.

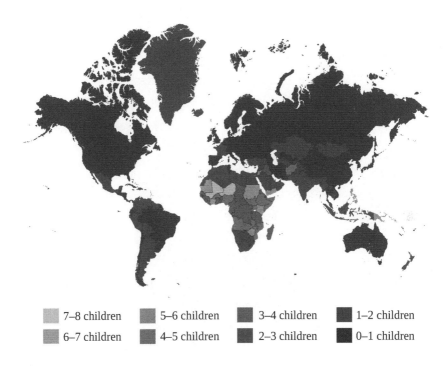

7–8 children	5–6 children	3–4 children	1–2 children
6–7 children	4–5 children	2–3 children	0–1 children

Source: CIA World's Factbook 2015 Data

Figure 1.1   World Map showing global variations in fertility per woman

Talent Pool in the US

U.S. job openings surged to a record high in July 2015[4], but slightly slower paces of hiring leads economists to suggest employers are having trouble finding qualified workers. The skills gap is a reality

5

many industries are facing. The labor participation rates are the lowest they have been in nearly forty years. In reality, I have experienced clients in Chicago subject to talent poaching in high tech industries and that has been taking place since 2014. The trend is already influencing significant wage increases to entice talent in the Midwest. Not to mention, the sometimes questionable practices of dipping into the talent pool of suppliers, customers, and businesses within close proximity.

There is no surprise the competitive talent sourcing techniques will continue. The generational gaps present in the available talent pool present a real threat in the coming years to 2020 (see Table 1.1). From the table in Table 1.1, the primary generations available currently in the talent pool are comprised of predominately Baby Boomers (born 1948-1964), Generation X (1965-1977), and Millennials (1978-1997). Generation Z (born after 1997) is only beginning to enter the workforce as high schoolers in 2015[5]. In the next five years, there will be a significant transition with over fifty percent (50%) of executives and/or seasoned talent retiring or seeking flexible arrangements on the road to retirement. This will result in a sharp decrease in the availability of seasoned talent and a large influx of young talent entering the available talent pool. With roughly 80 million Baby Boomers, 48 million of Generation X, and 78 million in Generation Y, there is a void of approximately 30 million in the United States. That is before you take into consideration regional, industry specific data and talent pipelines by education, areas of expertise and/or study. Compound that statistic further when conducting an age analysis of your current workforce against the time it takes to create your talent, vs. buy your talent specifically with respect to your sales projections and growth plan forecasts.

Table 1.1   Composition of US Workforce

	2005	2010	2015	2020
Traditionalists	18%	8%	0%	0%
Boomers	42%	38%	30%	23%
Gen X	22%	22%	22%	22%
Gen Y	18%	32%	39%	43%
Gen Z	0%	0%	4%	12%

Source: US Census Data

You need not be a statistician to realize the void facing us in the United States. One of the most concerning factors about the time frame set forth by the composition of the workforce in the talent pool is the fact that this significant shift is already upon us. Even more alarming however is there simply will not be enough seasoned talent to fulfill demand. Many do not realize, in fact, that even low wage earning positions have talent that will be sought after across industry, leading to voids in areas of industry that are not expected. This is due to the fact that all businesses, large and small, will be competing for the same limited pool of talent. Thus, talent will have broader options making it increasingly challenging for employers. While globalization is a reality in today's economy, many businesses are not open sourcing talent just yet. I would argue many businesses in the United States still source talent domestically. It is reported that between 25 million and 27 million small businesses in the United States account for 60 to 80 percent of all U.S. jobs[6]. The United States International Trade Commission defines a (SME) Small to Midsize Enterprise as firms that employ fewer than 500 employees.

Skills Gaps Hit Home

In recent years, the economy was a constant external factor affecting businesses. Many were reactive vs. proactive and the issue at the forefront of the economy was a shortage of jobs. This skills gap persists in many sectors. However, the shortage of trained or skilled employees and of low-skilled employees willing to work is doubly concerning now[7]. Patrick Doyle, the President of Domino's Pizza, says that the franchises around the country are having a hard time filling delivery and clerical positions. "It's a very tight labor market out there now." Anyone who has been sourcing or seeking talent must be aware of the misalignment that currently exists between the competencies required by industry and the skills of current job applicants.

Many would argue the way in which we work has forever changed. Not only is "office" a verb now, technology advances have shaped what we now refer to as the Information Age. The impacts on work and the way in which it is accomplished have been vast. Automation and off shoring impacted manufacturing and many jobs traditionally found in manufacturing were displaced through 2008-2010. Many companies, in fact, did not survive. That is how most of us remember it.

The current list of Fortune 500 companies contains more service companies and fewer manufacturers than in previous decades. The new demands from businesses require knowledge workers. What is a knowledge worker, you may ask? Knowledge work, can be differentiated from other forms of work as it places emphasis on "non-routine" problem solving that requires a combination of convergent, divergent, and creative thinking[8.] The segment of the population that has been displaced is faced with either learning a new trade to advance their skills or accept a low skill, low wage position. In a 2014 the Manufacturing Skills and Training Study published by Accenture presented the following question, "What percent of manufacturing roles require the following skills levels?" Thirty five (35%) percent of roles were for highly skilled positions; forty-five (45%) percent of roles were for skilled positions, leaving only twenty percent (20%) for unskilled positions. More concerning from the study was the fact that the majority of skilled and/or highly skilled roles are currently facing "severe" skill shortages[9]. Thus, there are not only skills gaps for knowledge workers but also in the skilled manufacturing trades. In 2015, I spoke at a Manufacturers Summit, among others and met Terry Iverson, President of Iverson & Company. His business has been a supplier to manufacturers in the Midwest for 85 years. He served on the Career and Technical Education (CTE) Board in Washington, DC and is also Founder of Champion Now. Champion Now (*Change how Advanced Manufacturing's' perceived in our Nation*) is a non-profit organization aimed at changing the perception of manufacturing in the United States. In an interview on my show, *HR in the Fast Lane*, Iverson explained, "In the United States we make nearly twenty percent (20%) of the worlds goods and yes, China makes twenty percent (20%) too but there is a reshoring effort to bring manufacturing back". The problem is that the jobs in manufacturing require retraining to keep pace with the advanced technologies. Iverson is an advocate for closing the skills gaps and pushing for math, engineering, computer, and even metrology skills among the youth. There are exciting careers in the field of manufacturing among others but even if we begin to retrain our workforce, the time and resource pool overall remains a factor. The United States is not alone given the global statistics released by Manpower, one of the world's largest staffing companies. Manpower has been conducting an annual *"Talent Shortage Survey"* for the past decade. Manpower Chief Executive, Jonas Prising stated in a video that accompanied the survey findings online, "The survey has covered a period long enough to include a global recession and constant technology and economic shifts." The survey sets forth the

Global perspective releasing the percentage of employers experiencing difficulties continuing to rise, increasing from 36% in 2014 to 38% in 2015. Hiring managers report the most severe talent shortage in Japan (83%). Around two in three employers report difficulty filling jobs in Peru (68%) and Hong Kong (65%), while talent shortages are an issue for (61%) of employers in Brazil and Romania. Many businesses in the middle market are without the resources of their larger counterparts. Yet, they will strive to be competitive as both small and large business, domestic or global in nature sources the limited seasoned/skilled workforce first. Seasoned talent will have the ability to set the stage for an open sourcing talent strategy as some will most certainly realize they are in demand and this is something many businesses have yet to contemplate.

Generational Influence

Another element impacting the looming crisis is the simple fact that the generational shifts in population present more than just a void in numbers. To be successful in attracting new talent, meanwhile retaining seasoned talent, poses an entirely new challenge to businesses. Every business and essentially those individuals that are tasked with guiding and leading people will require generational agility. The importance of understanding the ways we all approach work, let alone how we get motivated to learn, grow and evolve with the businesses, we serve will be critical. What appears to be a reasonable breakdown of a third of the workforce being Baby Boomers, and roughly a third being Generation X, followed by a third of Generation Y quickly shifts to Generation Y being the majority in 2020 (See Table 1.1). Overall the percentages reveal unique challenges but most concerning is the time in which this will all come to fruition. Many businesses have limited or have completely forgone their investments in training and development from the years of recession to current day. For nearly an entire generation, there have been plentiful resources and time to develop talent. Seasoned by experience, talent can take a decade or longer to achieve in any industry. What businesses face now are depleted resources, being either not enough talent or skilled talent and not enough time to develop the talent given the time allotted or the prior methods for which we have become accustomed. The impact to growth, productivity and in some cases entire industry in the United States is critical.

Compounding the numbers is not enough however. The simple fact is that people are not commodities and the generational cornerstones bring about complexities that are rapidly changing the way in which we work with one another. Clearly, one can expect generational differences but significant perceived variances are leading to tension, loss of productivity, communication breakdowns and potentially increased supply and demand struggles based on early integrations of Millennials into the workplace.

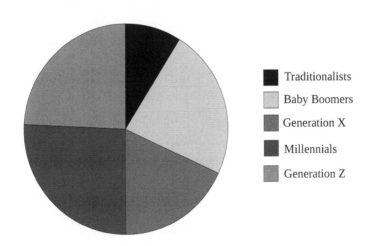

Source: US Census Bureau

Figure 1.2   Generations as Percentage of US Population 2014

Generational agility with respect to working with a diverse talent pool requires knowledge of the significant differences between the generations while building HR strategies that highlight the ways we are similar vs. the ways in which we are different. Before we can present potential solutions and strategies that build on a solid framework for success, we must understand the key areas impacting work directly.

Generational agility must be mastered with respect to understanding and adapting to the values that shape each generations' views. Significant differences present with respect to work ethic, training/career development, and incentives and rewards.

Let's begin with work ethic. One of the most obvious differences affecting workplaces today is that Baby Boomers literally created the fifty hour workweek where work ethic was in fact reflective of their worth. Working under Traditionalists, Baby Boomers learned from a generation where the company came first. As a generation, many were loyal to the workplace and were hesitant to take time away. Enter in Generation X, and no surprise, this generation has a clearer focus on work life balance and family. With a work to live mentality, however, Generation X was willing to pay dues and work hard as many came up conforming to the corporate ladder amassing skills that would lead to their next opportunity. Work ethic is important to Generation X but not as much as gaining skills. Thus they are most loyal to where they feel they will amass more skills and feel reward for their effort. Most recently, both aforementioned generations have learned the Millennials have a revolution all their own. Life is short in the mind's eye of a Millennial. While many think their value is work life balance it truly is more than balance of work and family. A Millennial has a global view and community involvement, self-development, and lifestyle is increasingly important. They will leave the office at 5PM. For a

Millennial, it does not matter where the work gets done, just that it gets done. They are responsible but will not sacrifice their lifestyle for their job. In fact, many see their Monday through Friday job as a side gig whilst they pursue their true dreams. It is seemingly a decrease in career ambition for the sake of a fuller more meaningful life.[10] This first variant between the generations has been stunning business owners and Baby Boomers alike and it is clear businesses will need Millennials more than Millennials feel they need them. In fact, in recent years studies have coined the Millennial generation the "entrepreneurial generation" but there are contrasting studies from Data from the Cooperative Institutional Research Program (CIRP) at the Higher Education Research Institute at UCLA, which has been surveying incoming freshmen at U.S. colleges and universities since the 1960s. Their studies reveal that Millennials are in fact less interested in becoming successful entrepreneurs than Baby Boomers were when they were the same age. The share of college freshmen that said "becoming successful in a business of my own" was "essential" or "very important" to them dropped from 47.9 percent in 1977 to 41.2 percent in 2012[11]. This finding does not change the fact however, that Millennials are tenacious and enterprising. A number of Millennials are in fact famous for entrepreneurship. To name a few, Kevin Systrom of Instagram, Mark Zuckerberg of Facebook, and David Karp of Tumblr, are in fact all Millennials. This speaks more to the fact that Millennials believe the best idea deserves recognition, not tenure, seniority or age for that matter.

Given we have skills gaps and little time to create skills given the rapid shift of human capital, how each generation views training and career development is imperative. Baby Boomers view skills as an ingredient to success but work ethic was far more important[12]. This poses a clash of values between Millennials and Baby

Boomers. The opportunity presents if a Baby Boomer understands that Millennials value training significantly. Millennials are eager to learn though it is important to note that mistakes are considered a learning opportunities. If a Baby Boomer sees a connection to being a part of what will create sustainability for the business as well as an ability to contribute to developing the talent and a path to reward all while overcoming that a Millennial will need to leave at 5PM, then a business may forge a winning initiative. It must be experiential learning strategically facilitated and brought into the workplace not for the sake of career ladder progression but rather competency development. Generation X can help buffer between the two contrasting views however it is important to remember that Generation X may have the opportunity to teach as well. The question remains as to whether the individual has the ability to teach in addition to the fact that if a better opportunity comes along for a member of this generation, they are likely to make the move. Often they are more loyal to themselves than to the business. Millennials are similarly dedicated to their development and they enter the workforce with more experiences than any other generation before them. Thus, they will seek more experiences and if they fail to realize it at work, they will seek it elsewhere. More Millennials leave work not for a new opportunity, but rather, they get bored.

This brings us to incentives. Businesses are surely going to need to revisit incentives to even begin to evade the looming talent emergency. What is sought after or valued by each of the three primary generations in the workplace today is different however. The one policy fits all frameworks are quickly going to become obsolete. Baby Boomers have enjoyed praise and typically will appreciate an incentive or reward that goes in the bank or on the wall. They appreciate rewards for their efforts and ideally the feedback would be face to face as relationships are important to them. Generation X is not nearly as enticed by material rewards as they are by freedom. Millennials seek to be part of something amazing. Thus, Millennials seek to be rewarded with a special assignment. Rather, consider tasking a millenial to take responsibility for a new initiative and take them seriously rather than delegate mundane or monotonous tasks. It is these differences alone that will require managers to develop generational agility and increased skills in providing feedback and developing relationships.

Women Remain an Opportunity

Another changing demographic is that females have officially become the majority gender in the United States in 2014. While women have been in the workplace in increasing numbers, the labor participation rate is lower than the US Population breakouts seen in Figure 1.3.

In fact, in review of the census bureau percentages we find that women made up thirty-eight (37.97 %) percent of the U.S. labor force in 1970 compared to forty-seven (47.21 %) percent between 2006 and 2010[13].

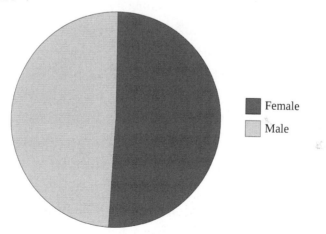

Source: US Census Bureau

Figure 1.3   US Population Male vs. Female

The change does not seem incredibly significant as many women entered the workplace to balance the economic needs of their families. In some cases women actually replaced vs. supplemented the income to their households through economic hard times. When looking to the future, what is more important is what can be done to improve the labor participation of women and what can be done to increase their interest in technical careers. It will continue to take time to close the gender gap let alone the skills gap.

Many organizations that are already faced with skill shortages today are taking proactive approaches to educate young women about opportunities in technical fields. Half as many women are working in technical professions as one might expect if gender representation mirrored the overall population according to Girl Scout Research Institute in a 2012 report. I would be remiss to not speak to some changes to impact culture as it speaks to women in the workplace. Specifically examples that come to mind include the nursing protection laws and the Lilly Ledbetter Fair Pay Act of 2009. Initiatives like these will not be enough to truly change as job sharing; work life balance or fully flexible work arrangements and equal opportunity for advancement have yet to be fully adopted across all industry and cultures in the United States. Of the women that are actively engaged in the labor force, a study by Harvard Business school published that sixty percent (60%) of woman work well past the birth of their second child, but ninety percent (90%) end up leaving not because they are pushed out or to care for their families but rather because of workplace problems, chiefly frustration and long hours[14]. There will need to be significant changes made in workplace policy and workplace dynamics for businesses to attract and retain women as a competitive advantage. Research from Gallup found that companies with more diverse workforces have a twenty-two (22%) percent lower turnover rate. The thinking being that if an organization has a more inclusive culture that embraces diversity that includes women, it will be easier to recruit a more diverse staff overall.

A Real Story: *TH Hilson*

Headquartered in the Chicagoland area and privately held, TH Hilson was founded with the vision of becoming a first class, family operated, progressive specialty chemical distributor and solution provider in North America. TH Hilson has expertise from the coating and ink markets, into metalworking lubricants, consumer care, adhesives, building trades, and plastics. I invited Lori Hilson Cioromski to share her real story as a female business leader and champion for young women seeking to advance in and enter into chemical, science and coatings industries. She is widely recognized for the proactive work in the industry and her results demonstrate her leadership is inspiring a demographic shift in industry. Her collaborative partnerships are a wonderful example of the ways suppliers, partners and customers in industry can partner for real results. Most recently she was inducted into the Chicago Area Entrepreneurship Hall of Fame, part of the Institute for Entrepreneurial Studies at the University of Illinois.

By Mrs. Lori Hilson Cioromski, President of TH Hilson Company

I was a very young girl when my father started his own business as a specialty chemical distributor. I never thought that I would be working in the family business so many years later. My dad asked me if I would consider joining the family business and after much consideration, I said YES, I would take the challenge and joined the family business after graduating from college.

Early on, I quickly realized that there were hardly any women in the industry; I was practically the only female calling on customers in the chemical industry at that time. I worked hard and was driven to succeed.

My Father provided a great foundation; he had the courage to turn the reins over to the 2nd generation, which allowed me to expand and grow the business to more than double his lifetime dreams. There have been struggles, challenges and celebrations since I became President. One question that I have often been asked is, "What is your proudest moment as a leader of your company?" This is a very interesting question and one that I have given a lot of thought to over the past few years.

I have to say that my proudest moment is how my employees pulled together during the downturn of 2009. During a crisis, unexpected downturn, when sales have diminished dramatically, this is when the toughest decisions need to be made. I let go of 13% of my staff, cut expenses everywhere we could and then asked all remaining employees including myself to take a 5% pay cut. One expense that I didn't curtail though was business travel expenses. I wanted my salespeople to be out in front of their clients, soliciting orders, working on projects and visible.

We took a hard look at how we were servicing our clients and re-invented ourselves during this downturn, which I like to refer to as my turning point. Because of the new direction we took, things got better and we were way ahead of the industry downturn. I was so proud of how my employees pulled together that I not only re-instated their salary, but I paid back everything that they gave up in 2010.

It was also during these difficult times that I got involved with the National Association of Women Business Owners (NAWBO) Chicago's Next Generation Outreach Committee (NGO) to help mentor young girls and women. I was committed to giving back to my community, even in the tough times, even when my company was having difficult times.

NAWBO Chicago's NGO Committee was asked by the Mayor of Chicago to participate in the Chicago Public Schools' Job Shadow Day. I thought to myself, my business isn't very exciting for a young girl, they would be bored if they shadowed me for a day. The chair of the committee told us that she wanted each and every committee member to participate and shadow 1 student for the day.

Believe me, I tried to say no, like so many times throughout my life, wanting to participate but too busy raising my family, running a specialty chemical distribution business, barely having a moment for myself. Does this sound familiar? I am sure that most of you can relate to this situation. But it was during this conversation that life was changing for me and propelled me to think outside of the box to come up with a creative way to show young girls the opportunities in the chemical industry.

My customers were doing some really cool things and I thought maybe I could take a student on a tour of one of my customers businesses. I made a few phone calls to some of my customers and found the perfect company that would be so interesting for the student. One thing lead to another and instead of providing a job shadow day for 1 student, my customer, Laurette Rondenet Smith, President of Edlong Dairy Products, brought in 28 female CPS students to learn about opportunities in the food industry. Together we were hoping to impact a young person's life in a profound way by giving them insight on how the roles of a chemical distributor interact with a food flavor manufacturer that provides flavors to the food producer.

The students learned about the sales process, created their own food flavors, and went on a plant tour to see the manufacturing and packaging process. "We are very excited about the opportunity to show students how our two businesses interact with each other to provide a broader look into how food products go to market. Laurette and I are both second generation business owners, members of NAWBO Chicago and are running successful businesss that aren't typically run by women. We want to encourage students to dream big and explore the possibilities that are available to them if they work hard and simply try." Lori Hilson Cioromski

Being creative and showing students real world examples of different career paths has been a big success. The news quickly spread of the career day we had and during a business meeting with the VP of Technology at Sherwin Williams, he didn't want to talk about the business we did together. He wanted to talk about having a career day in order to help attract new young talent.

In the chemical industry we are faced with experienced people getting ready to retire, without having the next generation to learn from them. It was difficult to provide awareness on the tremendous opportunities that are available to bright young people in our industry. Together with one of my top supply partners, Cabot Corporation, we had 57 students from Chicago State University visit Sherwin Williams to learn about the opportunities in the coatings industry. This was a useful tool to show young people what our industry has to offer.

What started out as a simple Job Shadow experience has turned into something so much bigger than I could have ever imagined. I am helping to bring awareness of the opportunities that are available to bright young people in the chemical industry, through career days, key note speeches and interviews.

In my business, we recently hired a young female salesperson and are having our experienced salespeople teach and mentor what they have learned over decades. The videos that came from some of the job shadow days have helped to provide an understanding of what the industry has to offer.

I encourage you to think of new ways to be the catalytic change in how you promote your business. Say yes to the opportunities that feel right with you and continuously look for creative ways to promote your business to the next generation.

Multicultural Workforce

The talent pool becomes increasingly challenging when you consider an additional element of cultural complexity. Leaders in every business are facing the reality of a diverse talent pool and workforce. The American workforce is more diverse than ever before with an added presence of young talent, women, and people of various backgrounds, faiths and cultural lenses. Those that lead people in their role will find it increasingly challenging with respect to communication and leading teams. As of June 2012, people of multicultural backgrounds (Asian, African American, and Latino/Hispanic descent) made up thirty-six (36%) percent of the labor pool, according the United States Department of Labor. Between 2000 and 2010, 7.02 million people immigrated to the United States from Mexico alone[15]. Our country has a long history of immigration and given our decreased fertility rates, immigration has in fact been strongly in force to augment the labor pool. Until the 1980s there was an influx of undocumented workers immigrating from Mexico and Central and South America. Of course, there had always been a mixed ratio of undocumented worker immigrants but in the 1980s it became a wholesale industry

21

according to economists. It is estimated that today there are 26.6 million legal immigrants living in America and approximately 11.3 million undocumented workers. The subject is highly political and there are a number of influences that have yet to be revealed with respect to immigration policy in the United States. Despite looming outcomes, the facts fuel our growing ethnic and racial diversity. By 2050, there will be no racial or ethnic majority as the share of Non-Hispanic whites will fall below fifty (50%) percent, according to Census Bureau projections[16]. Diversity used to speak to gender alone but in today's world, it speaks to being globally astute across geographies, races, family formations and cultural norms. This will impact competency development for leadership that many organizations have yet to develop let alone implement.

Source: US Census Bureau

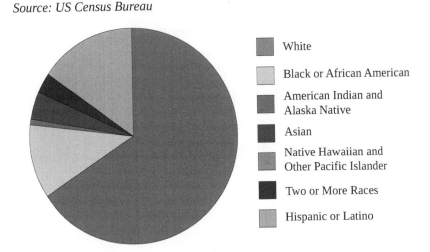

Figure 1.4   US Population by Race 2013

The worldwide competition for talent is one reason immigration reforms spark such emotional debates in the United States. National Security has the stage but skilled talent is a close second. While critics of more open immigration balk at allowing foreigners to claim jobs in the United States, those who run high-skill or technology enterprises complain that the best engineers from China, India and elsewhere end up in Europe or in rival nations because they cannot obtain the work visas needed to fulfill their needs[17]. Some businesses are going beyond satellite campuses to attract Millennials, and take the global step to open representative offices abroad for global competitive advantage in an effort to fill skills gaps. Establishing a proactive approach to the multicultural workforce is inevitable and though it will present its own challenges it has tremendous opportunity that far outweighs the potential constraints to advantage.

Most challenges that will face businesses with respect to a multicultural workforce include how we approach work, how various cultures view time and perhaps most important, how we communicate not only in language but behaviorally within the constructs of authority and respect. The competencies of the future will need to be strongly grounded in gaining awareness with respect to not only generational agility but cultural agility as well.

Clearly, the crisis has many ripple effects in business. The crisis is that only the top ten percent (10%) of CEOs are focused on building employee first cultures. There is a significant threat facing the business community and the talent emergency cannot be avoided.

Next, the **Realities of Change!**

CHAPTER TWO

The Realities of Change

If you knew me, you would hear me say, "it is not just the change but rather the transition". Often changes are rolled out with great enthusiasm but beyond the initial communications, there is much left to be desired. Earlier this year, my firm, HRBoost hosted a Culture Leadership Summit. All of the speakers were solid practitioners in their fields. Noting the fact that I genuinely believe in open collaborations and dialogues as we work through challenges we are to face given the *Talent Emergency*, I knew I desired a Keynote Speaker that would speak to the realities we all face with change. Change is constant and in business it is compounded by the rate at which we are experiencing change. Survey findings[18] report change fatigue as a common obstacle, with over sixty-five (65%) percent of respondents in the 2013 Survey on Culture and Change Management reporting change fatigue as a general lack of concern or passive resignation towards organizational changes by individuals or teams. Yet, we all know change is not to be avoided; some agonize, prolong or even become complacent rather than embrace change. A key to being competitive in business however is anticipating change and preparing for it[19]. Many businesses that I have worked with have trouble implementing a new technology with ideal utilization let alone a complete demographic shift rich with human dynamics. I can recall a President I once consulted for making an impulsive decision to purchase a $200,000.00 Enterprise Resource Platform (ERP). While there were shared convictions about the need to introduce technology there was a lack of consensus on which platform would be the best. Needless to say, without buy in at inception the system was still in implementation two years later. Note, when I say implementation, it was in stage one. This was a smaller organization, approximately $20 million in revenue and 100 employees. Imagine what this expense looks like in a larger organization?

In the example, I provide there were emotional components that led to the impulse purchase decision. The reaction from executives that were only briefly involved before the purchase led to the side barring of the entire project implementation as a result. Other examples that I often see are the tribal employee that has been with an organization since its inception, ridden the wave of high growth, only to realize the work environment has changed. Expectations often change, systems and processes are implemented yet people can and sometimes do clench to what once was. Coping and facing change are a reality in business today and often the changes feel like they are happening to us. Knowing every leader I work with must confront and facilitate change, I invited Brian Kedzior to be our Keynote speaker at the 2015 Culture Leadership Summit. At the time, he was the Head of U.S. Change Management for a leading financial institution based in Chicago, Illinois. It is a member of the Federal Reserve System and operates branches in the states of Illinois, Indiana, Arizona, Missouri, Minnesota, Kansas, Florida, and Wisconsin. This financial institution has over 600 branches and employs 14,500 staff in the United States. Kedzior led a team of eighteen professionals dedicated to change management. He has spent over ten years building change and what he calls "resilient change" connecting leaders. Given his expertise he was a wonderful presenter and helped highlight the importance of including change management in the solution equation. My personal favorite was when he shared a photo of his two young children and a personal story. His children have a routine to begin the day but one day he was able to be home from work so he and his wife thought it would be wonderful to surprise their children and go out on an adventure first thing. Needless to say, the children did not react favorably. Rather, they were visibly upset and ironically not excited about the plans for the day. The detour that ensued was something even Kedzior would have like to have prevented. Kedzior explained this example to bring us all to a place of awareness. We have all grown into adults and certainly have refined our visible reactions over time. Regardless of our maturity, age or wisdom, many of us will still feel the emotions the same way we did when we were four. We just may compartmentalize them differently.

The Time for Change Leadership Is Now

Today, the question for any business is if your business is resilient enough to embrace change as fast as the world in which it operates? With change fatigue being what it is, falling not far behind is waning commitment to change. And last but not least, many organizations have yet to implement bottom up initiatives strategically thus change initiatives continue to primarily originate from the C-suite. Please know I believe in executive support and sponsorship but for anything to truly be executed upon, it must involve the people of the organization. When Kedzior consulted my objectives for the Summit, we were quick to agree that there is a sense of urgency in today's business environment. Through our work we understand that getting everyone to adapt individually let alone as a team can be a monumental challenge. It is a fact that seventy (70%) percent of the changes your organization makes will not fully achieve the intended results. It all comes down to people. The human elements are dependent on being brought together and Kedzior argues this is done person by person. The emotional framework built through relationships must still be done with the person in mind. One of the key elements of his presentation focused on the differences between conversation and communication. Businesses may do a great deal of communicating but to affect the change necessary we all need to get better at real conversations. A commitment to change and ideally the approach whereby all feel genuinely part of the solution is the objective. Leader meetings need to be held in an open forum and not just in a presentation with a show and tell mentality. Team exchanges must be around real issues and not just a "structured ice cream social without true dialogue" as Kedzior likes to say. He was quick to share with our audience that people need to remember that any change can affect a feeling of loss. As humans he poses we are hard wired to have a breakdown in trust. That is part of who we are as humans. He proclaimed it to be self-preservation at its best. When leaders elect to truly bring a call to action, twenty (20%) percent will get in front and twenty (20%) percent may never adopt the change but bringing this level of awareness to the way in which we lead will be important no matter if you are a change agent like Kedzior or if you are the leader on the front lines facilitating teamwork between diverse members of a team in your day to day routine. One must bring people to a level of presence beyond being present. The simple truth is businesses cannot afford to have employees that come in day in and day out and feel "It is just a job!" Not only is this a disservice to the business, it is a disservice to the human spirit.

The number one broken element in business is trust. Some would argue accountability is a close second. Trust is critical to facilitating positive change however I consider trust to be a form of currency; truly it is cash for anyone that considers they are in fact a leader. It takes time, effort, authenticity, compassion, and honesty…even vulnerability but most important it takes a commitment to live the truth and be worthy of trust itself. Credibility is measured daily by peers, subordinates, and guiding mentors and the higher you appear on the management ladder, the harder it is to devote the time to build trust. Often we can be pulled away from the people simply tending to the task at hand. Leaders committed to building values as principles in the business not only take time to reinforce them and build trust, they develop many leaders that align personally and professionally to those fundamental beliefs.

I recently interviewed Tim Czech, Chief Financial Officer for Integrated Project Management Company, Inc. (IPM). I invited him as a guest on *HR in the Fast Lane*, an online show sponsored by Mabbly that I host on Advisor.tv in downtown Chicago. He credits the organization's success to the founder, Richard Panico who continues to grow a business on the foundational principles of quality, trust, and honesty.

Czech had attended a private event where Ted Garnett, the founder and Managing Partner of PS Culture Matters, LLC and co-author of the book, *Build the Culture Advantage,* teamed up with me to facilitate the game of SPEED. Garnett is known for his work as a Culture expert and he teaches that "Culture is not an event. It is a process. Lather, rinse, and repeat." Essentially the SPEED event is when leaders come together to play the game to win. During the game, a business simulation takes place. At the end of the game that Czech had participated in, it became clear that he was a true brand ambassador for IPM and most specific to their value of ethics. He literally got up from his chair walked across the room and stated to another peer leader in the room, "I would not do business with you!" Czech is rather soft spoken when you meet him so I know his action was driven with passion and conviction. Truly, one of the best portrayals I have ever had the pleasure of witnessing as a brand ambassador tied to the principles in which IPM was founded. I would encourage you to check out his interview with me to gain insights as to how they committed to a strong foundation for trust and ethics in leadership. There is no mistake why IPM, Inc. is featured as a Great Place to Work, featured in Inc. Magazine and has been honored with numbers more of accolades. They have committed to reinforcing their values from the culture invitation to the performance expectations and it carries through all the way to the customer. Without saying, it is in the people and who they are. Check out their featured contribution in Chapter 8.

High performing organizations measure manager performance based on their ability to create trust in relationships. One of best leaders I have the honor of serving directly links positive changes from people metrics to performance scorecards and bonus frameworks for leaders that work for him. There is transparency, accountability and a commitment to positive change in that the voice of the people is directly tied to the financial performance and payouts.

Have you measured trust in your organization? If you were to measure it, how much change do you feel is needed? Do you know where to begin?

The Evolving Field of Change Management

Given many will be dealing, coping, managing or finding themselves surrounded by change, it seems relevant and timely to provide a primer on change models. John P. Kotter is considered an authority on leadership and change. He has authored a number of books and for the purposes of this chapter, it makes sense to present a number of thought leaders who are published and are known for their change management models. When I was in graduate school it was about Organizational Development (OD). OD is a field that emerged in the late 1950s and early 1960 built on insights from group dynamics and from theories of planned change. Today, it remains among the leading integrated frameworks employing systems thinking and action research models for behavioral science interventions in business. I recall learning the Congruence Model for viewing the organization as a system. Inputs led into strategy formulated from people, informal and formal organizations with simple reference outputs for the system, then the group, and finally the individual. It was systems thinking through OD models and interventions to address organizational structure and theory.

It was actually later that Kurt Lewin became one of the first to conceptualize OD through action research models as the founder of modern social psychology. He focused much of his career on the development of force field theory, the unfreeze/change/refreeze change management model. The 'action research' approach to research, and the group dynamics approach to training.[20] Lewin believed that the motivation to change was strongly related to action. He mainly set forth that if people are active in decisions affecting them, they are more likely to adopt new ways. Lewin's three step change management model of *unfreezing, movement*, and *refreezing*[21] conceptualized that in order to begin any successful change initiative one must first start by understanding why the change must take place. As Lewin put it, "Motivation for change must be generated before change can occur. One must be helped to re-examine many cherished assumptions about oneself and one's relations to others." This is the unfreezing stage from which change begins. In contrast, Kotter presents his first step as critical and also handled poorly by most. His first step is known as *setting the stage*. He has published that the number one problem he has witnessed through his work has been about creating a true sense of urgency. Kotter's first step involves creating and sustaining a sense of urgency that helps others see the need for change and enacts the feeling of importance to act immediately. I find it to be even deeper however when you consider the emotional context of one's reaction to any new information. Imagine you walk into a room of people and present them all the same information, any information considered new but different then the norm. Will they all walk away with the same take on what occurred it the meeting? The simple answer is NO!

By now, you hopefully understand that traditional OD methods of change and organizational improvement as well as traditional change models, focus primarily on establishing a business need. From that need a team is assembled to define the change objectives. Solutions are identified and perhaps even new processes are presented to the workforce for integration and adoption. Kotter presented this as becoming "institutionalized."

Newer thought leaders like Jeff Hyatt and Tim Creasy release case studies, research and tools through the Center for Change Management. In their book *Change Management: The People Side of Change* they present the solid case for how a perfectly designed process that no one follows produces no improvement in performance. A perfectly designed technology that no one uses creates no additional value to the organization. Perfectly defined job roles that are not fulfilled by employees deliver no sustained results. Whether in the workplace, in your community or in government, the bridge between a quality solution and benefit realization is individuals embracing and adopting the change[22]. The tools available from the Change Management Learning Center PROSCI are resources that can be universally applied. Kedzior is certified in the PROSCI methodology however you do not need to be a change management professional to gain learning to be an effective sponsor of change. Managers of choice and leaders with purpose will be the ones to see their teams and businesses through the biggest shift in human capital history. There are five key goals presented in the PROSCI methodology known as ADKAR. They are: Awareness of the need to change; Desire to participate and support the change; Knowledge of how to change (and what the change looks like); Ability to implement the change on a day-to-day basis; and lastly, reinforcement to keep the change in place.[23] ADKAR methodology presented to the traditional change management world proposes that change happens on two dimensions: the business dimension and the people dimension. Successful change happens when both dimensions of change occur simultaneously.

I was having lunch recently with Neesa Sweet, Principal Consultant and founder of The Braided River Group LLC. Sweet consults as a strategist, coach and facilitator with expertise in change management utilizing insights from neuroscience and polarity thinking. In our conversation, Sweet noted that, while Change Management as a competency is in ever growing demand among business professionals, there are vastly different approaches.

Sweet identified LaMarsh Global, based in Chicago, Illinois, as a known pioneer in managing change. Their methodology, from the beginning, has focused on the individual being asked to change and what can be done in terms of communication, pacing, relationships, training and other tactics to help people align themselves with overall goals. This emphasis is in contrast to other forms of change management which are more project management focused. LaMarsh today offers both consulting and certification programs. A successful approach to change, Sweet noted, may be influenced by insights from systems thinking. In particular the idea that what happens in one part of an organization affects other parts; as well Organization Development, which emphasize the role of values and deep conversations in efforts to change.

While new approaches and models continue to emerge, says Sweet, one thing to remember when you are asking people to change is that everyone responds a little differently. Most people go through the stages that Elizabeth Kubler-Ross first identified and Dennis Jaffe and Cynthia Scott simplified to four stages—*denial, resistance, exploration and commitment*[24]. However, in Sweet's experience the reality is that people may skip around and backtrack when they are really under stress. Like

I emphasized in the beginning, Sweet agrees it is not just about looking at the beginning and the end—it is the transition in between. Sweet also pointed to William Bridges, who distinguished between *change and transitions—that things and systems can change rapidly, but people need to go through a transition period.* Some may do it faster than others, depending on their perspective.

Neuroscientist Evian Gordon first pointed out that the organizing principle of the brain is to seek reward and minimize threat. Usually, most people see change as threatening. There is an immediate activation of the neural system that responds in a fight or flight mode and shuts off the ability to think, reason, analyze or innovate. Which explains why Kedzior expressed we should expect it. Clearly, good change management is about helping bring people out of that state.

David Rock evolved the SCARF model—whenever people perceive their *status, certainty, autonomy, relatedness or fairness is at risk,* the threat response kicks in. What Rock has noted is that people can be helped through change by upping one of the factors if another is threatened. If your status is threatened by a merger, for example, more time spent with your boss (relatedness) can help you through the change.

Whatever model you are familiar with or choose to implement, remember it is people that must change to affect positive change.

Building the Culture Foundation

Simon Sinek has a simple but powerful model for inspirational leadership — starting with a golden circle and the question "Why?" His examples include Apple, Martin Luther King, and the Wright brothers. Check him out on YouTube!

The Employee Value Proposition = Unique Selling Proposition

The diversity from which all people are coming to work from presents the absolute necessity to get to the root of why? Not what, not how… but why? The premise of this is either agreed upon or not. If you were presented the why, you are either aligned to that truth or you are not. If you are not, then clearly you cannot devote your passions to build upon that change. If you are, then one can reasonably proceed to the next step. Ironically, it seems much of the communication taking place with respect to change can get lost in the "what" and the "how" without first establishing the reason. I would argue one cannot achieve a sense of urgency without the "why." As Dr. Henry Cloud has written, "it is the difference between pain with a purpose and pain for no good reason."[25]

I have had the pleasure to facilitate culture teams using PS Culture Matters framework which provides organizations a proven process and tools to leverage their unique culture and deliver sustainable performance with clarity and speed. As a certified partner, I customize the Accountable Culture Management™ process with my clients and obtain the "voice of the people" through a trend-based Generally Applied People Metrics survey GAPM™ tool made available from PS Culture Matters. When I work with my clients one of the first objectives is in working with the leadership team to identify strategic priorities and values. This requires defining the "why" in an executive alignment session as well as defining "success" and leadership perceptions which are later compared to actual metrics. The culture team cannot begin to align to a strategic priority without the "why" to inspire them and connect their action planning directly to strategy. No surprise, such an initiative can take a tangent when businesses need to align the executive team. I have found myself facilitating executive retreats in order to begin to gather the foundational inputs that culture team work is built upon. I have yet to encounter a team that includes the CEO and executive leadership to complete a *Culture Alignment RoadMap* (Figure 2.1) with inputs that are matched among two leaders let alone five or more when initially approached. The Roadmap tool was initially published in the book, *Build the Culture Advantage*. Often misalignment begins among the executive leadership realizing that what they thought was clear and communicated is in fact missing clarity and alignment as it moves through the workforce. Another observation I have from my practice with businesses is that many businesses are working on tactics in the Align or Manage Phases (see Figure 2.1) while having skipped the Define steps.

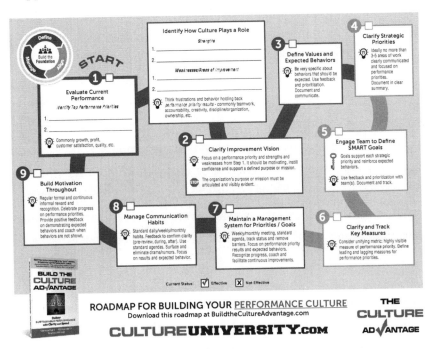

Source: Kuppler, Tim, Ted Garnett, and Tom Morehead. Build the Culture Advantage. 2014

Figure 2.1   Roadmap for Building a Performance Culture

In the best scenarios whereby the executive team is in alignment on strategic priorities, values and objectives can still be misaligned with the workforce. In fact, I would argue in most businesses the workforce is not aligned. Studies have revealed that only ten (10%) percent of CEOs ensure workforce alignment to priorities, values and objectives through strategic culture plans. In most situations, many feel they have communicated but much takes place day to day in the business to derail the message as intended. I recall one team I worked with this past year. We began in June and as I shared the top three priorities from the executive sponsor, a member of the team declared, "...it would have been nice to have known those priorities." You might be surprised to learn that this is in an organization that is committed to culture and it goes to show even the organization that is committed to workforce alignment must be committed to the continuous framework that it takes to reinforce core values time and again. *The Culture Maturity Model* is a framework that was developed to allow for quick evaluation against the journey any business will progress through on the way to becoming a high performing organization. For me it has facilitated in depth conversations with leaders of businesses that may already be recognized as an employer of choice but are still on the journey to achieving a high performing state both quantitatively and across all levels; self, team and management holistically. The difference between Culture Level 3 and Culture Level 4 can be seen when individual leaders may be achieving but when it comes to supporting key stakeholders and working as one team they remain segregated. Without silo segregation the individual can remain the key barrier to a high performing state (See Table 2.2).

In practice I have witnessed the impact of change being faced head on and perhaps even buffered by executive leadership with good intentions. Yet, when you gauge the voice of the people, the questions are raised as to the plan, the direction, and contingencies? People have a need to know and buffering only evades the opportunity awaiting the workforce. There are many questions from individuals once the work is done to create a safe exchange among the team. Employees can often experience a lack of understanding with respect to the intentions or even the bigger picture. Perhaps all have been addressed behind closed doors but until such time it is shared via a real conversation from leadership credibility is lost. Change initiatives, big or small, must be embraced in conversation be it in open forum or one on one. Even when this is done in the context of a culture team, it only presents opportunity and hope in the first cycle. Only with the repeated commitment to uphold the process and the conversations will the culture mature through solid relationships. It takes time especially in environments where workforces haven been subject to initiatives that were not carried through. Without this any change will feel like a top down initiative vs. a shared call to action.

OD change models and theories were built on initiatives that were led and supported by top management. I recall consulting a CEO on his merger and acquisition activity about a year ago. He believed in the importance of culture and yet he prioritized his strategic plan and operational plan first. When you are acquiring your competitor and the mix of each business unit comes with its own formidable culture, the strategic plan will not be embraced if the employees still feel that the acquired business is "them" not "us." How can two businesses merge to become "we" if we don't take the time to understand who each of "us" are? The desired change state cannot be reached without first identifying the current state. This CEO was confident in the communication and simply felt the strategic culture plan was one too many plans. That may be what would seem apparent but only qualitative and quantitative metrics can tell the true story. "We" does not just happen. In my experience, the business is more likely to succeed when simultaneously the business enacts a strategic culture plan. To forgo a strategic culture plan signifies risk to the strategic plan and operational plan success overall. It is that simple.

Table 2.1   Culture Maturity Model

	Culture Level 1 **Reactive**	Culture Level 2 **Functional**
Strategic & Financial Alignment	• Lack of clear priorities / goals & system for managing status & plans.	• Clear strategic priorities / goals & adequate system for managing status & plans.
Core Process Improvement	• Major pain managing many core processes. • Negative impact on employees & customers.	• Substantial pain managing some core processes. • Improvement clearly needed to reduce frustrations.
Motivation	• Major trust issues & a break-down of communication.	• Foundation of trust & communication. • Basic management recognition but improvement needed.
Talent Management	• Ineffective or limited talent management systems.	• Limited application of effective team structures. • Basic competency development & performance management.

Source: Kuppler, Tim, Ted Garnett, and Tom Morehead. Build the Culture Advantage. 2014

Culture Level 3 **Collaborative**	Culture Level 4 **High Performance**
• A motivating vision is effectively supported by collaborative priorities crossing functions or boundaries. • All levels understand financial drivers & supporting measures.	• Full Strategic Alignment with individuals, teams & the organization continually optimizing & innovating. • Financial drivers fully understood & clearly supported by relevant measures & goals at all levels.
• Effective core processes but streamlining opportunities remain. • Effective application of lean and/or other improvement tools.	• Efficient, innovative & marketleading core processes are continuously improved. • Advanced application of lean or other progressive improvement tools.
• Solid trust & communication systems. • Strong management recognition. Incentives at individual, team & organization levels.	• Deep trust & open communication exists at all levels. • Motivation & enthusiasm evident at all levels. Employees know they make a impact.
• A hierarchy of teams exists. • Clear performance management with feedback from multiple sources. • Solid competency development aligned with priorities / goals.	• Effective collaboration & teams at all levels. New hire fit assessed through teams & other approaches. • Fully aligned talent management systems with progressive development for competencies, leadership & succession.

A culture plan enacts the voice of the people and creates a framework for shared vision and involvement. Without the methodology of a strategic culture plan, people will simply feel what is being done to them and/or in other cases what they feel is being taken from them. Individuals are not likely to feel part of the solution unless there is a call to action that clearly speaks to them as individuals.

On the contrary, wouldn't it be better to have the people aligned to be part of the solution? If an initiative comes top down, it leads to people exhibiting behaviors that are not conducive to positive change. We have all experienced the co-worker that withdraws mentally, the gossiper that conspires and feeds the grapevine, and of course there are those that outright refuse to make the change. Resistance will occur and in worse case scenarios, manipulation and sabotage where severe distrust exists will ensue. This can be passive, in some cases even subtle, but make no mistake…it is toxic to the work environment. A toxic employee begins to build alliances with peers and the strongest personality in influence and presence wins. The lack of relationship from the executive leadership to leaders throughout the organization can pose significant breakdowns to workforce alignment. This is specifically challenging to leaders in large organizations with large teams and businesses with silo frameworks.

Managers of Choice

It is no surprise the competencies that managers need to succeed in the coming ten years are ever evolving. Businesses will not just need managers for traditional planning, delegating, monitoring and planning. Anyone trusted to attract talent, develop talent, retain talent in addition to ensuring it feels appreciated, yes appreciated, will need skills that make them managers of choice. Managers of choice are necessary to become an employer of choice. Managers of choice will know how to talent scout, skill build, relationship build, be organization brand builders and trust builders[26]. How many businesses have developed these competencies to their proprietary framework? Skills like these are unique to every business, every team and to truly be competitive they are built in alignment with the "why." For change efforts to be effective, it will take every employee to be viewed as a leader. It will take seasoned managers who are knowledgeable on mission, values and guiding beliefs to live and reinforce valued two way communication, guidance, coaching, and consistent facilitation. Managers must follow through to live the culture plan while implementing the strategic and operational plans. The "why" should inspire not only the executive leadership but every single person who dedicated their time and talents to its cause. Once that is universally understood, "what" must be done and "how" it will get done becomes intertwined with the strategic culture plan to ensure the integrity of the "why" is upheld, again and again, and again.

Facilitating change has become part of every manager's role. I read once that ninety (90%) percent of strategy is execution and ninety (90%) percent of execution is based on people. Doing it effectively and with skill is now the requirement for any successful manager of people. To be resilient or adaptable is of fundamental importance. Being proven in trying new things, embracing curiosity, being approachable and staying open minded are all equally important to enacting processes. Change programs or systems that create a framework for bottom up transparency and reward as well as opportunity for social exchange and shared learning are positive ways to integrate change and bring people in. Leaders that become skilled in these approaches will naturally create environments that others are drawn to. Collaboration is one of the top five metrics driving financial performance in businesses today[27]. Change cannot happen effectively without collaboration. Change management is not what I am thinking of in this context. I am focused on change leadership. Change leadership emphasizes the nature of change but also the human elements that are a reality where change is concerned. Managers that can facilitate and lead change, articulate the vision, inspire others to live it and support the consistent nature in which it must be upheld are tasked to be brand builders. To live it and uphold it not simply for the business but in alignment with a leader's personal joy and purpose.

Successful leaders can empathize that change is difficult and exhibit compassion but they must also commit their convictions to the need for results. This can be simple or complex. It is really in the eye of the beholder and their ability to engage in real conversations in a timely manner. I recall visiting a senior HR leader and she happens to work at an organization already recognized as an employer of choice. She shared how everyone was disgruntled about moving offices. We joked about the realities (never forget to have humor in your day) and when she asked for some advice, I thought it would be spontaneous to take flowers (as they had access to a floral shop they owned by coincidence) and either personally hand the flowers or plant to the person as they settled into their new desk and thank them for embracing the change. It was simple. Kedzior stated it well in his presentation by reminding everyone that we must all appreciate every impact of everything we do. Some may seem small and insignificant, but nothing is small and insignificant. Never underestimate the significance of being a positive leader from wherever you lead. By taking time to notice, you will make a difference.

Managers of choice will be required to have a more horizontal orientation to management and leading vs. the traditional vertical orientations from which many of us were brought up in. Crowdsourced Coaching™ is a technique that was developed by Dr. Jay Colker. I have had the pleasure of facilitating on two occasions with Dr. Colker and the applications of Crowdsourced Coaching™ are numerous. It is based on an educational model where an open forum group taps into the collective knowledge of the crowd to achieve immediate inputs and perspective that leads to greater impact and results. The technique leads to real conversations and by doing so it can engage leaders to building capabilities. Group collaboration can build a basis for a collaborative culture as well as more creative and innovative solutions. The technique is also great for shared learning which will be needed in businesses that are faced with accelerated timelines for development. The problem with the vertical orientation in leadership is that often the leader feels a burden of responsibility. They in essence own the problem and may even feel the need to be viewed as an authority. As a result, a leader with this orientation can begin to retreat from the demands placed upon them and retreat from the group vs. towards the group. Moving away from group goals to personal goals does not form a solid environment for coaching or collaboration. Dr. Colker's research[28] and his work with leaders internationally has presented the solid framework for the horizontal orientation of a leader. The horizontal leader is centered on tasks rather than on themselves and will put the team and others at the core of their focus. The focus becomes on the end goal vs. personal status and values include collaboration and contribution from the team. A horizontal leader will view teamwork as critical to success. Managers of choice will need to exhibit a horizontal orientation to help others shine and actively engage in shared accountabilities. Through my work with Dr. Colker I have seen firsthand the benefits through even one live facilitated session. He on the other hand has the pleasure of facilitating cohorts for weeks and/or months and cohorts can realize many of these additional benefits through a shared learning framework:

Feel accepted and a sense of being equal among others,

Accept myself and have the courage to be imperfect,

Share responsibility and work through others,

Have high social interest, high empathy, and a strong commitment to other,

Effectively contribute in the life tasks (work, social relationships, and intimacy.

Applications are endless in the field of change management, leadership development, and even human resources. The technique can be used by leaders to achieve results with any or all of the following areas:

Leadership alignment

Leadership development

Change management

Mergers and acquisition

Enhancing team effectiveness

Fostering innovation

Reinforcing cultural norms

Performance management and coaching

Cultural Competency

Cultural awareness will be another critical skill to the new age manager of choice. The nature of their curiosity and respect for another person on the team will help them to better understand the differences that should not hinder the team. This leader seeks to learn and understand why something is different that they expect. The idea is to assume difference vs. similarity. When you assume similarity you can be caught unaware of important differences[29]. When they approach the team member, they ask, "Why is that?" with genuine curiosity. Often the reply will bring about a new level of awareness and once realized, the leader can begin to coach vs. judge and ultimately enable an environment that can optimize the team. Today's politically correct environment can make a person feel hesitant to inquire but any person who cares to ask should expect and come to hope to learn from the answer. Assumptions are alive and well, practically commonplace in fact. Challenge leaders to learn about one another and provide an environment where cultural awareness is upheld with respect. Cultural elements can affect perceptions of respect for authority. This can be seen when team members are not overly participative to what we in the United States are accustomed. Traditional work environments have been hierarchical but Millennials have been gravitating to businesses with flatter structures or more egalitarian management environments. Egalitarian management styles are based in the doctrine of egalitarianism, a term that derives from the French *égal*, "equal"[30]. Managers with this style will seek to minimize the perception of power between themselves and their team members. In the same way, employees with managers like this may be more likely to feel comfortable questioning the manager. Managers of choice will be adept at "flexing" between styles and cultures to highlight what brings us together vs. what makes us different.

The key change facing managers in every business is the need to adapt and be able to adapt their style effectively with people of various generations, cultures, and individual strengths. This will require a different support framework with respect to talent development and high potential performer competency tracks. Change leadership, however, can become everyone's responsibility within an organization. This will be explored further in the chapter on organizational leadership. The bottom line with culture awareness, however, is how each manager of choice is trusted to guide and coach people to performance. This will mean managers must understand that approaching each person as a unique individual is required. Businesses have developed HR career tracks and career ladders that can send the message that one size fits all. This is no longer feasible if you are in the business of developing and retaining talent at the pace necessary to stay competitive in the coming decade. Each person will need to be met with their distinct learning style, personality, innate strengths and values in mind and in alignment with the business values and goals. This will require evaluating managers of people to a level of emotional intelligence and a level of unconditional positive regard (UPR), a term coined by psychologist Carl Rogers. A person that has the qualities of UPR employs an unconditional acceptance of others, even in their vulnerable and weakest moments. This is a key trait for truly seeing the potential in another person and working with them as they develop turning failures into teaching moments. Millennials in fact regard mistakes as learning opportunities.

By now it is clear 'change' has become inevitable in today's organizations. The needs of the organizations are changing and the ways in which organizations will be forced to facilitate change is now. In larger organizations like a leading financial institution, there are divisions for Change Management, Human Resources and even Leadership Development. In contrast, middle market businesses today may not have the internal resources to identify who their change agents are but, one thing is clear, someone will need to be facilitating change in every business. Next, we will evaluate the role of Human Resources as, not only has the role of HR Professionals been required to parallel the needs of changing organizations in the recent decade, there are many leaders of businesses who have not yet realized the value proposition from HR. Given the *Talent Emergency,* executive teams must begin to realize that without an HR infrastructure their strategic plans may not be realized.

Next, we must explore the ever changing **Role of HR!**

CHAPTER THREE

The Role of HR

From the looming crisis to the realities of change, it becomes clear there are compounding threats facing organizations today. We have touched on the importance of increasing globalization, rapid technological change, tougher competition for skilled talent; organizational changes such as new organizational alliances, new structures, the tear downs of hierarchies, ways of disseminating work, and a very high rate of change. There are evident changes in the workforce, including employees' priorities, capabilities, and demographic characteristics. Every business, be it a small team of 10 or an expansive workforce with thousands, has a need for and in many cases, an opportunity for the human resources (HR) function to play a critical role. To be embraced by leaders in business today, however, HR professionals will have to increase both their real and perceived value.

Coming up in HR

I can recall when I first was promoted into HR. I was one of 6,000 associates working in a global financial services firm, pre-Y2K. One may recall, when all the speculation gloom and doom was broadcast noting how banks would crash upon the turn of century. The first Employee Manual I ever knew was 5" thick and every aspect of decision making pointed to a process and procedure complete with signature authority ranking. I was part of what was then commonly referred to as the Personnel department. The uniqueness of my first role was that I was one of two individuals establishing a remote HR office for a satellite campus. While I had been placed originally in the role of onboarding and orienting newly acquired teams to their new parent company I learned rather quickly what not to do in HR. It was the late nineties and downsizing initiatives were becoming the norm. The realities of the role were clear and no matter my personal sentiments or lack of connection to the big picture overall, I was responsible for communicating bad news. After gaining my undergraduate degree and four years of solid corporate experience, I branched out to the middle market and took on my first management role in the field. From that point forward, I was fortunate to have always worked directly for a CEO. To this day, I feel that fact alone has played a significant role in my success in the field. Every leader I worked for after my experience in a large corporation allowed me to personally know the visionary behind the business. I learned each leader truly valued the people in their organization and was doing their best to navigate the labyrinth of employer obligations, external influences in addition to the natural dynamics of people working together. More often than not; all the while experiencing change and adapting along the way. I learned early not to be for the employee or the CEO, but rather for the business. It takes consistency, truth as credibility is cash and I found a commitment to clear communication is 99% of everything.

In the years that followed, I learned the importance of business asset protection. From my first Affirmative Action audit to I-9 ICE

Audits to employer response to EEO and DOL claims. Many in HR speak of compliance and what must be done. Ironically, what often fails in the message is the concept of how good prevention and proactive risk reduction makes good business sense. Employment is one of the most highly regulated and potentially litigious parts of running a business and yet at no time should leaders be paralyzed from making good business decisions out of the fear of being sued.

Soon the realities of benefits administration were before me. Anyone in the trench knows the complexities of benefits administration but from a business perspective, it means one thing to the profit and loss of a business; containment! Long term cost containment has led to wellness strategies, total rewards frameworks and now the concept of well-being is alive and well. I was fortunate to work in manufacturing environments. Highly diverse and skilled, such environments were a rich learning ground. In a poor economy, it was more important than ever to get the most out of employees. This was never about command and control; it was about reaching success, striving for the goal and developing organizational capabilities in real time. I have never aimed to implement a rewards program without understanding the competencies that drive revenue.

HR cannot possibly be strategic if it does not properly identify what is being done now to address the objective. The objective is tied to how the business derives profit. If this is not known, it is hard for the HR professional to speak in business language that resonates. It is critical to identify where time and money is being spent now within your respective functional area and role, especially if you are the leader of the department. It must be clear how time and money contributes to the objective overall in order to support a vision. I never allowed the potential value I could bring to an organization be stifled by inefficiency or ineffective results. Perhaps because I reported to the CEO, it was easier to befriend the CFO wherever I worked.

It is important to discuss with the financial minds on your team. A couple years ago, I spoke at a national conference on *"Linking HR to Profitability"*. A key portion of my presentation was to educate HR professionals to the fact that they need to befriend their CFOs. I actually follow CFO.com and read *The Economist Intelligence Unit Limited* reports. It is easy to cite the historical reputation of tension between finance and HR and yet I had to chuckle when a CFO I interviewed earlier this year asked, "…is it really true that CFOs and HR don't see eye to eye?" He had gained insights into this sentiment from attending the National SHRM (Society of Human Resource Management) Conference. It is sad to see the saga continue. Published articles from the Economist read "CFOs regard HR as "Strange Land" populated by "Strange Creatures" while "58% said their Head of HR was not the same caliber…does not understand the business well enough" and a final quote read "…only 30% thought HR was a key player, while 75% wanted to see HR play such a role." Mark Salsbury stated it best in his blog post, "Is It HR's Role to Support the Company, Or Its Employees?"[31] He wrote, "…for those HR folks who are still struggling to find their role within their organization, self-reflection through this lens is important to consider. Perhaps more important though is what others have to offer as an objective opinion. After all, as HR professionals often preach to employees during career advisory sessions, "perception is reality." Often if one is objective, it is easy to find the drain on expenses, time and productivity. The opportunity presents itself when you can strive to identify initiatives now that are not being done that could positively impact the overall objective. That may be to drive profit, create a revenue center, and develop capabilities tied to talent retention, managed turnover as well as business asset protection.

Many confuse HR tactics that canvas the employee life cycle. To name those most commonly referred to would include recruitment, hiring, compensation, benefits administration, payroll/tax compliance, performance management, workplace liability management, safety, records retention, technology (HRIS) and employee separation.

Strategic HR objectives are those that can drain, restrain and threaten profits when not managed properly. There are seven that I have come to know well. These are HR Expense Management (Short Term), Leveraging HR Time (HR Administration), Business and Asset Protection, Long Term HR Cost Containment (Health, WC, SUI), Turnover Reduction, Talent Attraction and last but not least, Employee Productivity. I would argue that most HR professionals do not speak about their initiatives, proposals and outcomes in these terms.

To deepen the language barrier, I will move into the areas of Profit and Loss for which every aspect of HR tactical or otherwise directly impacts negatively or positively. The area by which HR has an opportunity to maximize profitability is to increase revenue (customer growth) by maximizing turnover reduction, maximizing talent attraction and maximizing employee productivity. To protect revenue, HR must work with business asset protection in mind. This includes protecting the business' proprietary information but also considering the capability of the workforce as an asset and proactively building capability. Capability is unique to every business and one cannot know it without converging with the financial mind in the business. All development, incentives and programs should reinforce the capability drivers. Expense management comes into being objective about how HR is managing expenses in the short term. Often an external assessment can help you get an objective look at how dollars are allocated now in exchange for the value received. Cost containment is more of a long term view on controlling expenses internally and this speaks to mitigating external costs like health insurance and compensation compression with a proactive move to pay for performance initiatives vs. sustaining cost of living increases. Turnover reduction and prevention specific to those positions that are deemed capability drivers, mission critical as well as not easily replaced must be managed proactively. The coming years promise a talent deficit with respect to skilled talent. It is important to note that managed turnover is necessary. It is one thing to lose a highly valued, high-performing employee and quite another to lose a disgruntled, underperforming employee whose skills are outdated. People can be trained in new technologies but every business must evaluate how much time they have, the time it takes to create talent vs. buy talent and the make or buy ratio must be determined in advance. Indeed, the turnover of some employees may end up saving an organization more money than it would cost to replace that employee. The obvious point is that not all turnovers should be avoided—some should be proactively managed. Thus, not all turnover is regrettable. Metric data must segregate what is regrettable from what is in fact not and a strategic HR professional would have this discussion as a forecast and strategy planning session long before the turnover was a reality. Cost avoidance speaks the reality of lawsuits, employer liabilities and fines as they relate to government compliance. It is HR's role to ensure that every manager is trained on risks and obligations not only with respect to the law but also the organizational philosophy as it relates to values. This has everything to do with HR delivery and HR as a service and support thus enabling managers of choice to be more effective. When done well, HR is not just a part of the business but a fundamental partner in your business. Business productivity has everything to do with employee productivity and analysis of results, yields, and outcomes as they relate to each role in the business. This too cannot be done without converging with peer leaders in operations and finance.

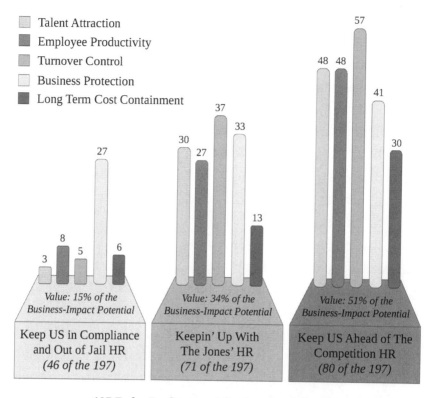

197 Tasks, Products, and Services that fall under
the Total Umbrella of Human Resources (HR)

Figure 3.1   The "TASK versus VALUE" Challenge in Human Resources

Competencies that Drive Value

Dave Ulrich is a published author and has written on the value proposition of HR for over a decade now. In his books he aims to set forth "actionable blueprints" as well as competencies for HR professionals and he provides a clear path to the next generation of HR[32]. He describes a multi-faceted approach to delivering HR services that meets the needs of both employees and employers, and positions HR as a significant contributor to organizational success. Ulrich presents his approach in terms of deliverables, or outcomes, for which HR should be responsible: strategy execution, administrative efficiency, employee contribution, and capacity for change. In the course of delivering in these four areas, he describes four corresponding roles for HR to play within a business: a) as a strategic partner working to align HR and business strategy, b) as an administrative expert working to improve organizational processes and deliver basic HR services, c) as an employee champion, listening and responding to employees' needs, and d) as a change agent managing change processes to increase the effectiveness of the organization. One of unique things about Ulrich's approach is that it includes all of the ways that HR can deliver value to an organization, rather than shifting focus from one area to another.

More recently, The Society for Human Resource Management, most often referred to as (SHRM), regarded as the largest association in its field, rolled out new competencies for all credentialed professionals. "Given where business is now, and where it's headed, HR has no option except to lead," said Henry G. "Hank" Jackson, SHRM president and CEO, at the start of the National Conference. "Our job is the most critical aspect of business. Finding, developing and keeping talent—that's our job. The stage is set for us to play a leading role in our organizations." HR must "focus on outcomes, not activities," he added[33]. The new SHRM Competency Model has been debated and there are many views with respect to the change. A great article from HR Executive online poses the "The Competency Question" that sets forth the nine competencies set forth by SHRM. Eight of them are behavioral: relationship management, consultation, organizational leadership and navigation, communication, global and cultural effectiveness, ethical practice, critical evaluation and business acumen. The ninth one is technical: HR technical expertise and practice[34]. The author contrasts the model against others as SHRM is not the only set of competencies available nor is it the only credentialing body for HR professionals today. There is also the HR Certification Institute (HRCI) that announced that HRCI had partnered with the RBL Group in Fall 2014. For the last 25 years, Professor Dave Ulrich and his colleagues at Provo, Utah-based RBL Group have been conducting the *Human Resource Competency Study*, a highly regarded, recurring survey that's been used as the basis for formulating a set of competencies for the profession in curriculums at large. The latest model from the RBL Group outlines six HR competencies: credible activist, strategic positioner, capability builder, change champion, HR innovator, and integrator and technology proponent. It seems HR professionals of the future will have a choice to certify with both, with SHRM, with HRCI or none of the above. I personally have credentials with both at this time but only time will reveal which certifications are continually regarded as the highest standard for HR professionals around the world.

Managing Talent Today with Tomorrow in Mind

The basis for managing talent today with tomorrow in mind is my way of speaking directly to confront the simple fact that employers at large believe their employees are in fact their most important asset. It is comical. If you were to ask anyone you know in finance or accounting to define an asset they might explain an asset as a useful or valuable thing, person, or quality and then they might go on to explain an asset can be bought and sold. Clearly, people cannot be bought or sold and yet in the coming years, many will operate their businesses under the impression that the highest bidder may in fact win the talent over. In Chicago, the talent poaching has begun and I have witnessed rampant career transitions taking place between customers, suppliers and competitors as skilled talent becomes increasingly desirable and less available. Many will follow the immediate increases in pay but every employer must know that pay is not a primary motivator. By the time a candidate accepts an offer for increased pay, they made the decision to leave their employer and it had nothing to do with pay. It had to do with their heart and mind. Often employers fail to deliver a work experience that offers an engaging high performance environment that keeps one's heart and mind in alignment with the strategy of a company and the personal values in synergy with organizational values.

Effective talent management can mean the difference between being an employer of choice or an organization that systematically hands off talent to the competition. How? You might ask. Well, actively reviewing turnover metrics and analyzing key areas can reveal trends that could lead an organization to a serious talent shortage.

At last year's awards symposium for the Best and Brightest Companies to Work For™, I exchanged business cards with a CEO being recognized. He had a quote printed on the back of his business card. It read, *"We have no patent on anything we do and anything we do can be copied by anyone else. But you can't copy the heart and the soul and the conscience of the company." Howard Shultz, CEO Starbucks*

It immediately presents the sentiment of any employer of choice. If you fail to start with the people that are entrusted to represent your company brand, how can your organization tap into the loyalty of a customer?

Engagement is the entire buzz but I would argue it is not the entire buzz. In fact, the word engagement does little to truly speak to the comprehensive metrics returning ROI to high performing organizations today. In the field of human resources, it is hard to be active in the field and not come across the topic of engagement regardless of the fact that is only one metric contributing to high performing organizations. Ironically, I still find myself walking into businesses today that will ask why they should care about engagement. Let's review a few statistics...

- Cost of turnover can be 70% to 200% of an employee's annual salary.

- Studies report companies with high engagement enjoy 3x the operating margin[35].

- Engagement and involvement are critical in managing change at work; **9** out of **10** of the key barriers to the success of change programs are people related[36].

- I don't know and I don't care. **69**% of US employees are either "not engaged," or are "actively disengaged." While 31.5% of U.S. employees are engaged, there are organizations that have doubled this number, perhaps most notably the Gallup Great Workplace Award winners. These organizations excel in their employee engagement strategies and they have realized substantial increases in engagement levels as a result[37].

- One factor that has been rated as the most important has been the extent to which employees believed that their senior management had a sincere interest in their well-being. *"Companies that understand the link between wellbeing and sustained engagement – and take steps to implement wellbeing strategies to support engagement – will have a healthy, productive and motivated workforce committed to the workplace, no matter what the economic climate."*[38]

HR leaders must play a significant role in driving both qualitative and quantitative dashboards with respect to the workforce. The danger in simply surveying the workforce without understanding what is being measured or why is that an HR leader could risk being perceived as the leader that confuses engagement and employee experience with happiness. Job satisfaction and happiness are again results derived from a number of factors that should be measured. Many businesses lead with scorecards and dashboards and if you have a HR department that is not well integrated, there is no time like the present. The emergency is often revealed in your metrics when you move away from time to fill and progress to quality of hire or time to full productivity. Compound it to truly look at how long it takes to make talent vs. buy talent and what ratio is necessary when you correlate those figures to sales forecasts? Critical capabilities must be understood and timelines for talent pipelining those skills is crucial. Often the numbers are small when in percentage view but the impact can be significant. Effective leadership is a key factor in employee well-being and leadership rating scores can relate to variable incentives for leadership. I have one client that ties his employee qualitative and quantitative results for leaders on management incentive directly to their bonus scorecards. Specifically, compensation trends are showing pay for performance finally coming of age but are the behaviors you seek to encourage part of the success? Other metrics that you can consider as you tie performance to business results include pull through rates and "activity based pay." Often, I witness businesses only measuring sales forecasted jobs awarded but no team incentives built in for awarded vs. shipped. One need not over analyze or over engineer metrics, but you must partner with Finance and Operations to really know the Key Performance Indicators that can fully integrate with the wealth of data being collected in HR. Much of this is trial and error and seeing what really makes sense for the business is the opportunity.

It may be helpful to review analytics models. There are four basic elements to human capital analytics systems. They are Assessment, Planning, Execution and Measurement. Every HR department is well grounded and likely concentrating efforts in the Descriptive context.

The Descriptive context is usually a single data point reflecting what has happened. The opportunity is to be proactive and gather additional data, taking in the external forces and then the qualitative inputs of the internal factors to begin to assimilate the Predictive analytics for your department. This is when you play out "what if" scenarios that estimate the probability of the "what if" scenario. For example, we measure engagement to ask a rating on what is the likelihood of talent leaving. I suggest one should take it a step further and ask, what capabilities would be impacted if this person were to leave? To be predictive in your analysis, you must be asking critical planning questions to yourself? For example, how will this evolve as business and workforce requirements change? Second, how will the source of change affect the workforce requirements? Every business is changing workforce requirements based on technology today. How does the rate of change in your work environment affect your ability to attract and retain talent?

The objective is to move your Descriptive analytic data to Predictive analytic data. Posing results that are not what happened but what may happen. When one has gathered enough inputs to correlate causal and historical data, you will be ready to make recommendations that are Prescriptive. HR has the opportunity to move from lagging indicators to leading indicators. Examples of leading indicators include trust, loyalty, readiness, engagement, and organization or employer brand. Yes, these leading indicators are believed to be intangibles. However, when you drop them in a logic model you absolutely can begin to put metrics that are meaningful around them. In my experience, the metrics that can offer the most value to the teams I have worked with have been the result of collaborative planning. This requires key questions and exchanges not only in the present state but the future state. What is predicted to change and how will the source of change affect the workforce requirements? Which are our mission critical skills? What skills and/or competencies actually drive revenue? What is in the sales forecast and what skills will any newly awarded works require? What is the incumbent's growth potential? Not just from what is thought but assessed and validated for strengths and cognitive ability to determine capabilities. Some believe it is all about potential. Current bench strength (how do we define strength in your business) and if the bench is not strong....what key stakeholders must you partner with to get it strong? How much time do you have?

How long does it take to source but further than that, for the hire to actually reach break-even point and deliver services in terms of competency that is required? How are you measuring this?

Measures that are leading indicators include: Readiness level of backups for key positions, Leadership rating by employee, Peer and Guiding roles, Engagement levels correlated to Performance/Productivity measures, Mission Critical Turnover rates and Time to Full Productivity.

It is necessary to embrace the will to create employer brand that aligns to the vision of the business. If HR strategy is not integrated with business strategy complete with links to core ideology that is reinforced time and time again, then what is HR reinforcing? The role of HR will be to create an invitation that speaks to brand ambassadors. HR must source and develop leaders. Everyone is a leader. What does it mean to be a leader at your organization? Commit to accountability and link to Key Performance Indicators. Link every HR tactic to the Profit and Loss of the business. And last but certainly not least, create continuous and automated feedback loops. When you get to Prescriptive Indicators, this is when you are measuring the leading indicators that drive strategic decisions whereby your HR data can significantly impact the strategic direction of a business.

A Real Story: *Radio Flyer, Inc.*

Radio Flyer is an American toy company best known for their popular red toy wagon. Radio Flyer also produces scooters, tricycles, bicycles, horses, and ride-ons. The company was founded in 1917 and is based in Chicago, Illinois. I have invited Amy Bastuga, Vice President of Human Resources at Radio Flyer, Inc., to contribute a real story. I have had the pleasure of knowing Amy for years through my affiliation with Best and Brightest Companies to Work For™ and her presence on behalf of a winning organization and shared best practices. Amy is a strategic HR leader who brought her expertise to an iconic organization whose vision was to create an innovative environment where every employee could say "I love my job." She has helped lead Radio Flyer to achieve recognition as a best place to work. She was the lead culture architect and initiated the development of strategic engagement programs and top notch talent acquisition practices. She has successfully established best in class development programs through *Wagon U* and championed a #1 rated internship program.

By Ms. Amy Bastuga, Vice President of Human Resources, Radio Flyer, Inc.

Radio Flyer needed to attract top talent in order to meet the vision of becoming the world's most loved children's brand. (We were like many companies faced with competitive pressures and growth challenges and we are all competing for the same top talent.) We needed a long term approach to a very urgent and immediate talent gap. We approached the challenge by focusing on several key areas:

1 **_Attracting Top Talent._** _Radio Flyer did this by building a_ **_culture_** _where talented people wanted to work, by promoting our_ **_employment brand_** _externally and by developing a_ **_pipeline_** _of talent through our #1 rated internship programs._

2 **_Retaining Top Talent._** _Radio Flyer did this by focusing on_ **_onboarding_** _(education to help Flyers connect to other Flyers, the brand and the business), creating a well aligned_ **_goals_** _process (education to help Flyers see their connection and personal impact on the company goals), and engaging Flyers through our culture building_ **_committees and events._**

3 **_Developing Top Talent._** _Radio Flyer did this by building our talent internally through the creation of_ **_Wagon U,_** _our internal learning and development courses and by establishing a Flyer driven_ **_career development_** _program._

The Human Resources team partnered with internal leaders and external expert resources to align best in class practices with the unique Radio Flyer culture. We have built a strong award winning foundation. It is essential that we build a talent pipeline and grow our talent so that Radio Flyer can continue to **_bring smiles to kids of all ages and create warm memories that last a lifetime._** _We have a special iconic legacy to protect and by focusing on excellent people practices we will continue to create a great culture that will allow us to hire and retain the right people who will build Radio Flyer for the next 100 years._

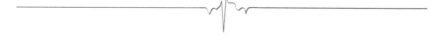

HR never works alone. This is why we will explore the value of **Team Engineering** next!

CHAPTER FOUR

Team Engineering

Have you ever wondered what motivates people? Why they make the decisions they do? Perhaps you are like me, someone who reads behavioral and psychological white papers for fun? Even if you are not, you have surely worked with someone that frustrates you, challenges your natural way of communicating and perhaps you feel you will never see eye to eye.

According to Merriam Webster, *complacency* is defined as an instance of usually unaware or uninformed self-satisfaction. Many would like to claim they have not been complacent. Yet in the workplace, I would like you to ask yourself, "Have you ever been in a meeting and bitten your tongue or held back something you naturally would have said simply to speed a meeting up or to avoid conflict?" If the answer is yes, then I would argue that you have been complacent in your relationship to a peer at work and perhaps even to your leadership responsibility. The value of diversity and constructive exchange is critical to innovation in any workplace environment. Yet, many will have become complacent in their relationships among stakeholders and peers at work.

The Evolution of the Job Model for Performance

It is a fascinating subject and given that I have worked on the human side of business my entire adult life I have witnessed this behavior many times. In an effort to resolve breakdowns in relationships, I have used many tools and facilitated team building exercises, workshops and retreats to include the use of assessments in an effort to bring people together. One of the first necessities of team building, let alone team engineering, is self-awareness. Without self-awareness and appreciation of one's own innate strengths, one cannot begin to appreciate the contrasting strengths of another. Only with personal knowledge to one's own self-awareness can a person align to purpose and values. The hard part of self-awareness is that it is personal and thus not something easily forced upon another person.

My own curiosity has driven me to experiment with behavioral assessments that have been available on the market. Some of the first I had exposure to in practice was during graduate school. Many of us are familiar with them and may have had personal experiences taking them. Common ones include Myers Briggs and DISC. To put it all in perspective, however, there are thousands of assessments available today. Popular ones I have enjoyed working with in the past had presented four-quadrant frameworks and theories. These always were entertaining and enlightening in improving communication when well understood. At minimum, facilitation for a team can take two to three hours and yet the question remains: How often are the findings of an assessment taken back to work in practice? Does it actually enable a person to be more successful in their daily practice with their co-workers? Will the assessment improve our evaluation or strategic hiring initiatives? Will it improve our bench strength?

I have found that over time the findings in earlier assessments are not always effective beyond the individual. Unless the organization canvassed the workforce with the assessment and truly supported a common language for all to embrace in their day to day practice at work, the benefits of such assessments can be quickly forgotten.

The best assessments teach you something about yourself. Something you may not have already identified. Many are raised to strengthen their cognitive abilities and traditional schooling is dedicated to the development of our IQ. When you begin to appreciate your own strengths in a way that is truly unique to you and only you, you can begin to appreciate those behaviors that are not among your strengths. The best assessments are not just personality assessments. The latest assessments measure cognitive abilities which directly correlate to job performance but also identify innate strengths whereby an individual can achieve a sense of joy and purpose in their work building on their strength vs. the cost and energy expended trying to "fix" a weakness.

I was fortunate to meet a man in 2013 that enlightened me to the big world of assessments. Chuck Russell is a nationally recognized thought leader in the application of assessment technologies to business practices. Naturally being interested in the roots of psychology, I took time to learn about his tools and began using them in my own practice. Russell wrote a book called "Right Person, Right Job" and in the forefront he poses "Today, the use of assessment information is no longer an option. The legal environment demands it. Maintaining a competitive advantage requires it."

Table 4.1   Generations Chart

Generation	Characteristics of the Generation	Assessments
7th	Cognitive abilities included Hard-wired personality traits (Big Five model) Normative scores Solid psychometrics Designed for business use Specific job behavior descriptions Requires no special training	BestWork DATA QueueMapper SalesMatcher JobThoughts
6th	Cognitive abilities included Hard-wired personality traits Normative scores Solid psychometrics Designed for business use Virtual interview text Requires no special training	CheckStart Factor 5
5th	Cognitive &/or personality traits Normative scores Requires consultants or special training or uses older profiling or benchmark methodologies	Prevue Hogan NEO-5 Harrison Profile XT
4th	Normative scores Universally accepted personality trait model Primarily clinical or professional use Solid psychometrics	MMPI 16PF

Generation	Characteristics of the Generation	Assessments
3rd	Mixed item formats Simple personality types or proprietary models Often tied to books or proprietary training	Myers-Briggs (MBTI) Caliper Birkman StrengthsFinder Devine Inventory Hartmann Judgment Index Herrmann Brain Dominance
2nd	Forced choice (Most - Least) items Simple personality styles Ipsative scores Cannot compare individual results Cannot create norms	TTI Tri-Metrix McQuaige DISC RightPATH
1st	Adjective check lists Simple personality styles Easily faked	Culture Index Predictive Index Omnia PDA

Source: Russell, Charles. About Assessments. Feb. 2015. Web. 8 Feb. 2016. Reprinted with Permission.

That was back in 2003! He is a passionate leader that has pioneered the use of new assessment instruments to differentiate elastic and non-elastic performance competencies, which has led to the production increase of 20% or more across a broad range of industries. For nearly a century we have all believed in the two-part model for job performance. The model was based on one part being for Attitude, Values and Motivation and the second part being Experience, Skills and Education. When faced with performance problems, this model was the guide for how to understand the cause.

If experience and skills were deemed acceptable, then motivation must be the problem and the answer was to motivate employees with incentives or with consequences. Sometimes that worked, but many times it did not.

If employees were motivated and performance was not satisfactory, the answer seemed to be training. Sometimes the training worked but sometimes the learning curve ceased to end and the training did not seem to make a difference. For the first time in the 1990s, serious psychometric instruments were developed specifically for the purpose of correlating job performance with hard-wired personality traits and cognitive abilities. Assessments that measure cognitive abilities have redefined the way businesses can evaluate talent to place the right person in the right role. This research has made it possible to see if an employee has the particular strengths and abilities to perform any specific job behavior. The qualitative evolution of assessments is something many outside the field are simply not conversant in. I have included Table 4.1 that Russell has developed and it is intended to provide a frame of reference by which a business can select the most appropriate tool given their unique needs. He originally published it in his book back in 2003 and has strived to keep it current[39].

It is important to note however that the selection of the instruments in the table is by no means a comprehensive listing. In addition, Russell presents that all instruments are good for certain purposes, and no instrument is ideal for all purposes. It presents some of the most popular assessments that are known with a generational overview as to what they measure. Special considerations must be given to how assessments and/or competency based tests are applied when evaluating potential candidates for hire. Best practices would suggest that the approach for each position be consistent and standardized. In addition, if an assessment is used to evaluate potential candidates, it must be directly related to job performance. If any business is considering the use of assessments as part of their standardized process, I would encourage a current review of their desired process against the Civil Rights Act of 1991, Americans with Disabilities Act of 1990 and the Equal Employment Opportunity Commission. It is important to note, however, that every governing agency is created to limit bias as it relates to prejudice and bias in the decision-making process.

After years of research, it has become clear that people might be able to do one job extremely well, and yet be completely unable to perform another one. Similarly, people can play some roles on a team, but no one can play all roles well. Thus, each individual strength against the critical factors for any given functional role be it management, sales or service (and hundreds of roles beyond these) can be evaluated.

Most talent is evaluated based on skills and experience but which skills are critical to any given role? Some may define competencies or demonstrate abilities in prior work. With a 7th generation assessment, any business can delineate the critical factors from the important. It is the critical factors that the ideal candidate must possess for ideal placement in any given role. I have learned a simple sports reference that may shed light on what I am speaking to. Imagine a baseball player. Now many of us have watched baseball. What are the critical factors for performance for a shortstop? Remember, these would be deal breakers. The player either has "it" or they don't! You might think of a number of factors affecting performance: Fielding grounders, catching pop files, throwing to first base, batting, running the bases, wearing the uniform correctly, perhaps even encouraging a pitcher or teammate. Now which are critical to winning the game? Fielding grounders, catching pop flies and throwing to first base would be deemed critical. Meanwhile, further consideration one could reason that batting and running bases are important but not critical as even the best miss from time to time and are still quite good. And then finally, wearing the uniform correctly and encouraging the pitcher are nice to have but not essential to winning the game.

Team engineering becomes a real opportunity for any team. Change takes a catalyst and nothing works better than a contrasting view. One thought leader I have come across, Gary Hamel, has published that to invest in genetic diversity is one simple way of overweighting every team and decision making body with individuals who are "younger than the company average, have worked in other industries, and are not based at the head office."[40] Team engineering is whereby we gain data and insights into the specific action[41] and behaviors that are directly correlated to behaviors like leading, innovating, learning, communicating and planning. Furthermore, we are able to identify the culture topology of a team as behaviors are closely tied to strengths. If you ask an Industrial Organizational psychologist how values are separated from behaviors, the answer will be that it is very difficult to separate a behavior from a value from a strength. An individual's values are essentially the strength expressed in the form of a behavior. People may learn the same skill but how they execute on that skill will vary based on their innate strength and how that strength is expressed in behavior. It is in fact, the variable that will impact job performance.

Interviewing techniques for selection are for the most part subjective in nature. Furthermore, the risk of expense for a bad hire from both the employer perspective and employee perspective often has lasting emotional and financial impacts. By the time the reality of a bad hire is realized, months or even years could have passed. It is important to note that a bad hire is not always a poor performer per se, but rather a person whose innate strengths were not favorable to the critical factors for performance in a given role. Most have experienced the expense and frustration not to mention the anxiety and impact to productivity when the old two-part model is the only consideration for explanation with respect to performance. The foundation of the performance of any team is found in the hard-wired traits & abilities of its members. Russell's research and work points to a clear and undeniable finding. Personality and cognitive ability are more directly responsible for performance on the job than motivation or skills or experience. Russell sets forth a new paradigm for the Job Model and the evaluation as it relates to job performance. He poses that **Company Fit** (attitude, ethics, and values), **Skills Match** (education, experience, and skills training) and **Job Fit** (how well an individual's cognitive abilities, personality traits and interests match those required for success in a given role) are the "cornerstones of job performance." Russell presents in his published works the degree to which talent does not fit is in fact the gap in performance. It is this gap that businesses must address with training or coaching or even by changing the job. The ideal candidate, however will "fit" in each area of criteria in the new three-part model. Many leaders I have had the opportunity to meet and work with put emphasis on Company Fit; that being culture fit, value alignment and many assess this fit subjectively through behavior-based interviews. Assessments that evaluate Job Fit and are balanced with evaluation of Skills Match and Company Fit are likely to achieve success in terms of job performance but also with respect to a feeling of joy and satisfaction with their task execution. Purpose is another element that is critical when accessing any talent's discretionary effort but that is expressed more qualitatively through workforce alignment of personal values in relationship to organizational values.

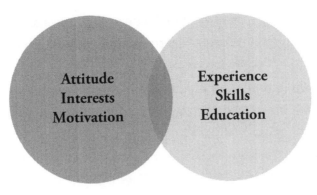

Figure 4.1   The Old Model of Job Performance

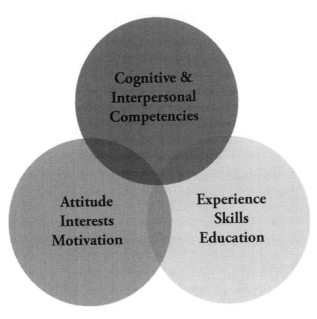

Figure 4.2   Today's Model for Job Performance

Source: Russell, Charles. "Team Engineering." Lecture. Reprinted with Permission

Team Engineering in Practice

Team Engineering is when a facilitator provides a full description and mapping of the group's complete ecosystem. With the data captured by a 7th generation assessment tool, you can engage a team on issues of management, collaboration, performance, communication or quite literally anything related to people and their behavior. It includes tools for the team leader, showing how each person will contribute to the team and how to bring out their value within the team. There are tools for each team member showing them how to be more effective within the team and with the team leader. These workshops are ideal for any management team or other type of work group where collaboration and communication is critical. Often, I facilitate leadership retreats whereby I integrate team engineering and often I find leadership then seeks to implement team engineering across their organization and various teams. On an aggregate level, you can see a baseline of culture topology, something I call "Culture by Default." I will review this more in part two of this book.

What I have found in my work is that team engineering reports allow people to take what they learn back into their daily exchanges within the team. I have also found the process to lead to strategic hiring decisions when in fact it is revealed that the bench strength is void of strengths that would in essence add to the value of diversity on the team. Far from being conceptual, the BestWork DATA, a 7th generation tool I have sourced, produces real results that become part of everyday work practices. When I work this into a retreat, it is a highly interactive program that easily expands into other areas of engagement and bridges to topical areas of leadership development. For businesses that seek to bridge generations, evaluate job fit without skills and experience inputs. In essence accelerate a team to performance with the assessments of today to enable the businesses of tomorrow.

I had a CEO contact me a few years ago. He was experiencing frustration with his plan for succession as well as with his management team. I had the opportunity to develop a custom retreat for his team but the first phase of the program offering was Team Engineering. To interpret the following table, I will share with you that the leaders were assessed with a 7th generation tool and then plotted on a chart whereby one can assess the strengths and diversity or lack thereof as well as gain insights into the challenges presented for that team given those findings. The menu of job behaviors becomes a common language for describing team roles and responsibilities as well as a variety of strengths that teams require to be successful. It is a language that is accessible to everyone with BestWork DATA. The Team Engineering Chart I have selected presents the team strengths inventory as well as highlights the Team Leader with an (*) asterisk.

The Team Leader is ultimately the person the team reports up to in a traditional sense. Thus, the Team Leader may be a lead, supervisor, manager or facilitator on an organizational chart. This team was experiencing significant communication breakdowns and it was no surprise once you have the DATA before you.

Table 4.2   Company "A" Team Engineering Chart

Indirect with feedback & calling out issues		2	2	1	5*	1	Direct with feedback & calling out issues
Does not challenge or offer ideas		2	2	1	5*	1	Challenges & offers ideas
Focuses on immediate issues				5*	2	4	Focuses on strategic issues
Little or no planning; reactive	1	2		2*	6		Detailed planning
Low need for details	1	2		2*	6		High need for details
Makes exceptions to rules & procedures	1	3*	1	3	3		Follows rules & procedures

Innovative thinking	1	3*	1	3	3		Conventional thinking
Slower information processing			5*	2	4		Quick information processing
Individual Effort for team	2	1*	3	4	1		Team-focused effort
Patient	4	5	1	1*			Urgent
Listens more than talks	9*		1	1			Talks more than listens
Quiet enthusiasm	9*		1	1			Outgoing enthusiasm
Little or no people interaction	9*		1	1			High people interaction
Behavior A	10%	15%	25%	25%	15%	10%	Behavior B

Source: Martin, Nicole. Company A Team Engineering Chart. 2014 ed. Vol. Client. Print. Leadership Charts.

The bottom three rows reveal that the majority of the team was concentrated in the lower percentile (15% LOW). This does not mean these people do not talk or are not social. Rather it demonstrates a lack of diversity in communication style among the team but also the reality that the majority will not expend the energy to communicate proactively. Many would think the one person who is to the higher end of the percentile (15% HIGH) would be the one that harmonized the team but in reality this person adapted to the dominant behaviors among the team and the team was surprised to see this person had such a strength that was hidden among them. Gaining this insight into the hard wiring of a team is enlightening even for the best teams I have had the pleasure of coming to know. This chart brought the team awareness as to the spectrum of styles, preferences and behaviors innate to their team. How people adapt their styles based on context is important. Understanding these interdependencies takes a commitment to flexing your leadership approach to bridging the gap with those on the other end of the spectrum. The more a leader is conversant in adapting their innate strength to communicating effectively to another, the greater the bench strength of the team and thus the competitive advantage of diversification.

Direct vs. Indirect Communicators
Expressive vs. Contemplative
Task Oriented vs. Relationship Trust Building
Individual vs. Team Focused Effort
Innovative vs. Conventional

This particular company realized not only their strengths but their voids and only then was the team able to develop strategies to work together to address the voids. Often the DATA alone is not enough to accelerate a team to high performance. Team Engineering is the beginning of team awareness and the way in which the team strengths can bring value to one another. What comes after is in fact the real opportunity. See, the boxes may not seem like much segregation but for a person to adapt to another individual just one box equates to not much conflict. It is feasible in daily communications. Not everyone will be one box away from their peer key stakeholders on a team. An individual may not have to expend energy to interact with a positive outcome to another one box away. When you look at another variance, however, a two box gap equates to significant stretch factors for an individual. The more distance one individual is from another, be it a three box gap or greater, equates to difficult challenges that can present and may require a conscious awareness to alter for another. Meaning, both individuals would need to establish a level of self-awareness as well as awareness of their counterpart's strengths and then adapt to meet in the middle. This must be accomplished with awareness and if all team members are hired for job fit, this reality is often the case as the person that is favorable to critical factors for financial roles will not possess the same strengths as the individual that is favorable to critical factors for marketing or sales roles. Yet, among leadership teams you are very likely to have the leadership from both at the table and within the same team. Other tensions this team observed were the number of individuals that would prefer to be told what to do vs. prefers to be the individual that delegates and prefers to tell others. Can one who is most direct listen to others? That is the variable of skills, experience and attitude. The answer is, yes. A direct individual can listen to others but this person would require experience and training to manage people effectively when being direct to an extreme in the (10% HIGH) or (15% HIGH) quadrant. Other questions this team engineering session posed were, what needed structure? What needs flexibility? Six of the individuals on this team will be more conventional and will follow rules in a similar way. In contrast, however, four will have rules but they may be fuzzy and vary from situation to situation as they make decisions circumstantially. To whom does it cost energy to collaborate to share information? All on this team were creative on a thinking line but there is a variable to creative. Understanding for example, who can create from nothing vs. the ones that prefer to edit the way that something looks? Clearly, the insights gained were of great value to the team.

The framework for Team Engineering sets forth the possibility that any team can gain insight into how truly diverse the team is. Often we make judgements that people are like us when, in fact, they may only be similar in one area of behavior or strength. The level to which a team is homogenous can also pose potential risks. Thus, achieving an awareness level of how a team is engineered is a foundational advantage to strategic planning and execution. A team can, in fact be engineered and when done with shared leadership in mind, the collective group can excel.

The EQ Quotient

Emotional intelligence often is referred to as (EQ) and though it has been studied and written about since the mid-20th century, it only became popularized following Daniel Goleman's book, *Emotional Intelligence - Why it can matter more than IQ?*[42] The Harvard Business Review called emotional intelligence (EI) "a revolutionary, paradigm-shattering idea." Essentially, Goleman presented that relationships and competencies like empathy and compassion can trump IQ in terms of success. He has spoken publicly to the fact that he can have a room of CEOs in a room and ask them how many graduated college and only three hands emerge. He presents that people with a 160 IQ are working for people with a 100 IQ. Clearly, IQ is not everything. Goleman presents that cognitive abilities get you in the game but it is the EQ that gets you ahead. Many of us learn what to do and that is IQ. Yet, through your life it seems only real experiences, face to face exchanges and deep reflections dedicated to personal self-awareness and mindfulness are known to develop one's EQ. Emotional intelligence is developed when we learn how to do versus what we do.

The best part about EQ is that is can be learned and built upon throughout our lives. I find the base of team engineering establishes foundational self-awareness and team awareness in a common language. However, the teamwork that can take shape after the foundational awareness is in fact dependent on EQ. Relationships are built with the cornerstones of empathy and compassion. Goleman presents three kinds of empathy. The first being cognitive whereby I can embrace where you come from. It is the golden rule we all learn.

"Do unto others as you would have them do unto you." The second kind of empathy is emotional and social. Goleman describes it as the ability to sense through feeling what others feel. It is more intuitive and a deeper form of empathy. The third kind he describes is the "basis for compassion" and he refers to it as empathic concern. This level of empathy is demonstrated in competency when a person sees another in distress and desires to nurture, to help. He describes it as the ancient mammalian brain most evident in parenting. I present Goleman's framework for compassion and empathy because now we all can begin to build our relationship skills to care enough about our team members, our peers, and our stakeholders in business. We must all realize that it never matters what we are doing at work, it all comes down to how we do it. How do we go about planning, deciding, communicating, and leading? Do we do it with EQ working in conjunction with IQ or have we become so focused on task that EQ was left behind?

Servant Leadership vs. Shared Leadership

Many regard servant leadership as an ideal in leadership, but within teams that are engineered, there is a higher level to aim for when it comes to engineering the team. Shared Leadership. Servant leadership is accomplished on an individual basis. The two concepts are very different. All leaders make a choice to serve others or use others. In essence, an individual makes a conscious choice to serve others vs. use others. When an individual makes a decision to serve others, he/she puts the needs of themselves behind others. This reflects in behavior characteristics like respect and appreciative inquiry. The individual actually takes the perspective of walking in the other person's shoes, being empathetic but also organizationally aware. See, it is not about wanting to help those less fortunate than ourselves but realizing one's kinship to another person on the team. To be organizationally aware is to realize by serving others you serve yourself. Servant leadership requires high emotional intelligence and leading by example. Servant leadership is considered a timeless concept; but it is important to note the phrase "servant leadership" was coined by Robert K. Greenleaf in *The Servant as Leader,* an essay that he first published in 1970. A critical takeaway from his work is that while traditional leadership generally involves the accumulation and exercise of power by one at the "top of the pyramid," Greenleaf believed servant leadership to be different. The servant-leader not only shares power and expertise but helps people develop and perform as highly as possible[43]. The servant-leader supports the organization and removes obstacles with awareness that the people who are closest to the situation know the most. A conscious decision by an individual within the servant-leader framework means consciously knowing I am not the best person to lead every initiative.

In contrast but on a similar spectrum is the concept of shared leadership. Shared leadership is a collective approach and truly comes from an organizational leadership perspective (Chapter 6). A team approach requires passing the work responsibility whereby a team must shift to adopt and optimize the team strengths to achieve high performance. Shared leadership must be engineered and designed. Team engineering is among the first steps for which organizational leadership is made possible. The distortion of what a leader is prevents the concept of shared leadership from being realized in the mainstream. Leadership development is largely viewed as an individual path vs. a collective path. The biggest misconception is the difference between leadership and management. The management model has always been presented as a hierarchy. Leadership is inverted as it is about serving and it should not be reserved or regarded within the hierarchical framework. Management and leadership should not be used interchangeably as they are two different disciplines. The opportunity of team engineering is the framework for appreciation for the team. Further understanding and development can lead to awareness of the peer stakeholders and the diversity of strengths as well as innate expertise within the organizational structure. It is this awareness and appreciation that gels on a collective plane and presents for the hallmarks of a high reliability organization. This inside out perspective is the basis for how leaders must support the workforce in order to serve customers. There must be more empowered leaders among the team to reach the customers. This has been fundamentally presented in the case of service excellence but the foundation of service excellence begins with shared leadership. Carl Albrecht was among the first thought leaders to present the Service Triangle, an inverted triangle that places the customer at the center with strategy, people and systems as three fluid and interdependent corners of the triangle[44]. His concepts were presented over 30 years ago and yet we all have experienced a service experience as a customer whereby the person serving us was restricted by some administrative procedure or system that inhibited service excellence. To ponder why this continues comes down to a simple fact. We have not trusted in people and provided a shared leadership opportunity whereby they are empowered as leaders to deliver service excellence. It is important to note that service excellence is not only an external ideal but an internal ideal as well. Often, the internal customer in the process or hand off of work is overlooked and this again comes back to team engineering, awareness and appreciation of peer stakeholder. This is not to be confused with concepts of teamwork or participative management. Rather, an engineered team must have complementary skills, be committed to a common purpose, have shared performance goals and an approach for which they are mutually accountable. Only then can shared leadership be realized. It is what separates groups from teams[45].

The way in which we are now able to engineer teams and support them in identifying their diverse innate strengths will dramatically change the way we consider approaching shared leadership from the inside out. Leaders who engineer teams given innate cognitive behaviors paired with evidence of emotional intelligence will be hard to refute when the reality of culture is, in fact, the "we." Who we are when we come together is the beginning of culture and if we establish "we" without inherently understanding the way in which each of us come together, the culture becomes a culture by default vs. a culture by design. Many businesses operate with culture by default while others excel with a culture by design.

A Real Story: *Medinah Country Club*
GM/COO Mr. Robert Sereci

Medinah Country Club is a private country club in Medinah, Illinois, with nearly 900 members and 640 acres (260 ha) containing three golf courses, Lake Kadijah, swimming facilities and a Byzantine-style clubhouse with Oriental, Louis XIV and Italian architectural aspects. Medinah is widely known for its Course 3, now at 7,657 yards (7,002 m),[9] which has hosted five major championships, three U.S. Opens (1949, 1975, 1990) and two PGA Championships (1999, 2006), as well as the Ryder Cup in 2012.

Contributed by Tammy J. Napoli, Director of Human Resources

All successful companies have leaders that excel at their jobs and bring outstanding skills to their organizations. That does not mean, however, that they have great leadership teams. The level of success and the ability of an organization to rise to the top of their industry depend on the cohesiveness of the team. It is that cohesiveness that drives the culture and sets the stage for greatness.

So how is team engineering different than what we already know about teamwork and the value it has to an organization? Let's take an example from Medinah Country Club, one of the most prestigious private country clubs in the US and in the world for that matter. In March 2015, the Club hired General Manager and COO, Mr. Robert Sereci to lead the Club through a renewal of service excellence and development of a winning culture. Mr. Sereci had a clear understanding of the importance of building a cohesive, aligned, motivated and hard-working group of leaders and the solid foundation for future growth and excellence they could provide.

After only nine months and through the leadership's participation in a team engineering workshop, led by CEO Nicole Martin of HRBoost, the Club leadership team is realizing a new energy and a true culture transformation. "The team engineering workshop took us to a new level of excellence," states Tammy Napoli, HR Director. "The leaders learned to work together in a way that leverages not only each other's strengths but individual styles, tendencies and preferences. The workshop taught us how to identify our key stakeholders and to create an action plan to influence them. It gave us the tools to see each other through a clearer lens and to move forward as a truly great leadership team. As a result, the services and manner in which we provide them to our members is truly exceeding expectations and reinforcing the tradition of excellence that is Medinah Country Club."

In part two, we will explore the ways businesses can align their business strategy to their strategy on building human capital. There is only one input that can threaten, restrain or drain a business as easily as it can maximize profitability. That input is that people and individual culture, group culture and organizational culture all depend on a business's investment in culture by design vs. default.

It must all begin with an invitation. Something I express as the **Culture Invitation!**

PART TWO

Culture by Default vs. Culture by Design

"If culture was a house, then language was the key to the front door, to all the rooms inside."

—KHALED HOSSEINI

CHAPTER FIVE

The Culture Invitation

In recent years, I have had many conversations with leaders and there are various views as to how organizational culture evolves. By simply asking, "Does culture come from the top down or the bottom up?" debate will ensue. In my experience, it is up to the visionary leader and/or the strategic leadership team to define what I call the "culture invitation." The framework for culture is as strategic and essential as the (Organizational Purpose) Vision Statement, the Mission Statement and the organizational strategic priorities. Unlike the Vision Statement expressing to the **Who (the internal and external audience)** the **Where** and the **Why**; the Mission Statement sets forth the **What** but the Culture Invitation expresses the **How**. The culture is the values, behaviors, beliefs and unspoken assumptions that are perceived and real in practice. Without a defined culture invitation, each individual will resort to their own personal behavior expression. It essentially comes down to what your employees feel and what your customers believe. Culture is as much internal as it is external. The invitation is, in fact, the employee value proposition and it is as important as any business' unique selling proposition. Or as I have read, "successful brand harmony requires an entire organization to work together in pursuit of shared goals"[46]. Steve Yastrow is a sought after branding expert that I had the pleasure to meet back in 2006. He was the Keynote speaker at the 101 Best and Brightest Awards symposium in Chicago. Thus, over ten years ago, the message was clear. He proclaims, "To have any chance of creating Brand Harmony, we have to aim much higher. We have to look at internal marketing as some of the most important and serious marketing we have to do... If your employees don't understand and believe in your brand, there will be no chance that your customers will be able to understand it"[47].

Words or Behaviors

Often companies have values expressed in the form of words vs. behaviors. Not to mention, the process in which values come about can be extremely varied. The bottom line is that if it is not reinforced time and again and in alignment with personal value expressions, it cannot be lived. Even Enron had core values like Ethics and Integrity and we all know what happened to Enron. Stating a culture invitation is not enough. Like anything, people must feel it and believe it. Organizational culture is characterized by its employees thus it can be branded but unless it is believed and felt by the employees, the organization will not have brand ambassadors. It is by default when it is not shared. Shared core values means the organizational values, whatever they may be, are intrinsically aligned to the employees' personal values and reflect the essence of the "we" among the "many". Thus, allowing each person to identify a meaningful role in feeling empowered as a leader from wherever they are in the business' and connecting them to the business' organizational purpose. Defining the Vision, the Mission without a Value and/or Belief framework negates the opportunity to achieve a transcendent organizational purpose. Without this, a business will not be built to reinforce the **Why!**

When this is missing, the workforce is unable to connect their efforts intrinsically to something greater than themselves. For example, a brick layer can go to work every day and stack bricks, spread mortar, stack bricks, and spread mortar again and again. It can be monotonous work that becomes drudgery or he can be empowered to know his employer builds homes that shelter a family within a community. He can know that his efforts every day builds homes and every home is not a place but a feeling.

The word invitation in and of itself speaks to the action of inviting someone to go somewhere or to do something[48]. An invitation relies on a mutual exchange and reciprocal expressed acceptance. This is critical. If an organization simply expresses an invitation but then the workforce essentially declines the invitation through behavior, then a business must ask, what framework exists to uphold the invitation and reinforce it as an expectation? Words are not enough.

Shared Values

CEOs tend to agree that culture is important but many still run their businesses expecting managers to manage people. The fundamental truth however is that managers should manage process, drive results and invite people to join them. People will, in fact, manage themselves to what is measured. The invitation is the framework by which they align or misalign. If they are misaligned, the business must ask if this is a process problem or a people match problem. Tony Hsieh, the CEO of Zappos.com, has an organization with a culture that is certainly unique and harmonious to brand. His earlier business led him to the leader he has now become. He has been cited saying, "Without a sense of shared values and some basic rules for working together, people can easily forget they are part of a team and start protecting their own parochial interests"[49]. Unfortunately, I have witnessed this in practice in every business whereby the culture invitation is not defined, measured both qualitatively and quantitatively. Research has shown that businesses that are good at culture are proactive about recognizing behaviors that are great. What may surprise you is that these employers are equally as proactive at recognizing great performance as they are at addressing poor performance. Effective leaders are just as focused, if not notably better, at recognizing performance and behaviors in the workplace that are not on target. Highest rated organizations recognize behaviors that are positive immediately after they learn of it. If a leader takes too long, the recognition can actually become a de-motivator. A second factor to recognizing positive performance is that effective leaders tend to tailor their recognition to the best needs of the employee. This goes back to knowing the appreciation language of the talent. Some prefer recognition one on one, others in a public format and even knowing what is valued by each person is the opportunity. Last but not least, the effective leader encourages others to recognize colleagues who do a great job and live the values. When employees are asked to rate the statement, "My manager identifies and handles performance problems in the early stages," the rating in the best organizations was significantly higher. Furthermore, other surveys I have seen will ask employees to rate the question, "I work with quality people" and this too is an expression of whether excellence is upheld in selection and performance management. The take away here should be that it is not only the manager that is responsible for culture. Once the culture invitation is expressed, handbooks, performance management, evaluation systems, career pathing and recognition programs directly linked to values and results are foundationally aligned. When this is done well, anyone in the business and especially peers can enact positive reinforcement though peer recognition programs[50]. As businesses grow, the shared values are upheld by the workforce and leaders across the organization must share the vision and then be empowered to model it and invite every employee to live in the expression of it. Communication must be clear and it must be tied to the Vision, the Values and the strategic priorities. The better an organization is at framing this in terms that every employee can understand, the better they will do in establishing trust and collaboration among their employees. The time it takes to define the Culture Invitation is what is often skipped, especially in high growth businesses. The reactive nature of business is something I have come to know well. I would suggest taking time to be proactive and framing the culture invitation earlier. If a business has a strategic plan and an operational plan, I would ask, where is their culture plan? The defining moments in clarifying the Vision and the Mission and then redefining strategic priorities year after year requires review of the qualitative and quantitative indicators. Without this, a business may become unbalanced between efficiency (short term thinking) and effectiveness (long term thinking).

Entanglement Versus Engagement

I have had the pleasure of working with Dr. Ray Benedetto in recent years. He and his partner, Steven Fallek together founded GuideStar, Inc. As a team, they have accumulated over seventy years of combined service through various leadership and management positions in business as well as in education. With the publication of the book, *It's My Company Too!* Co-authored by Dr. Ray Benedetto, they have sharpened their leadership development programs to focus on practices for *Character-Based Capitalism.* Their practices help executive teams create *organizational entanglement,* where employees act as owners, use discretionary time for critical thinking, and generate new ideas that drive innovation, productivity, and growth. Their work demonstrates that leaders need to align individual performance with organizational expectations for ethical performance, which is difficult if financial returns represent the sole measure of business performance. In his experience, many business leaders fail to recognize the critical role organizational culture plays in company success. Their thought leadership has demonstrated the importance of organizational leadership. An organization cannot truly transform from a culture by default to a culture by design without organizational leadership. This will be presented in Chapter 6. With respect to the culture invitation, however, their research has coined a term "entangled" to represent a unique magnetism that draws employees together in high-performing character-based cultures that strengthen relationships through which they collectively attack and solve "sticky" issues[51]. The term "entanglement" was coined to represent these phenomena. It includes the following employee attributes:

- *Employees think and act like owners;*

- *They live and breathe the company purpose;*

- *They focus on gaining the best possible results for all stakeholders;*

- *They continually engage discretionary thinking to solve complex organizational challenges; and*

- *They understand how collective attributes of the company transcend individual goals.*

Clearly, "entanglement" is beyond "engagement." One area of culture that is often misunderstood is how important it is that the workforce is involved in decisions impacting their work. I remember when I participated in the 10,000 Small Businesses® program back in 2014 we had to bring in a cultural artifact. Essentially a tangible object was requested and I found myself troubled with the assignment. Culture is not tangible in my mind. As my small business began to grow, I found there was a clear delineation between my expressed values, which essentially became our service ideals, and the beginning of the "We" that was taking shape that is now our core values. My boutique consulting firm is small with on average up to fifteen employees. This highlights something I know and many leaders experience. Culture can vary with 19 feet of separation and in some cases, even less with private offices and high walled cubicles. Thus, the instant your workforce expands beyond that measure of distance and is no longer an intimate office environment, the Culture Invitation is imperative. Knowing the importance of connecting personal actions to company purpose and the desired culture, I elected to embrace the "We" through a facilitated exercise during a team retreat. I enacted a survey whereby behavior expressions were listed in words and each employee opted for the values they identified with. I did the same but highlighted my response as their leader and then separated those results. I expressed my top values and then we baselined the values of "We" the people. Only the values that were truly in alignment, overlapping and essentially lived in practice, became the "We" that is in fact shared. I share this because had I come top down with the values and belief statements, they would not be "We," they would have been "Me." I chose to outline what was non-negotiable as service ideals. Those ideals are values that were already in existence upon establishing my business. They were, in fact, my sentiments expressed to our clients as well as my team. They are in essence the brand promise and also present the deal breakers when it comes to service expectations. They are more external facing whereas the values speak to the intrinsic beliefs in how we do what we do, day in and day out. They have an opportunity to be truly lived because we created them together and now they are expressed as the culture invitation for any future talent that may join us and elect to align to our organizational purpose. If an employee does not believe in the value and belief statements, they will know immediately upon review of the value expressions. Whether they align to our organizational culture or not, it is clearly expressed so that talent will be able to self-identify and align or deselect prior to onboarding. I take on the responsibility of recognizing those in alignment to our service ideals and performance results as they impact our client commitments. This may be delegated to operational leadership as a business grows and in truth inevitably should. The team, however, has the responsibility of proclaiming their individual and team or departmental performance. They are empowered to live the culture and highlight who they feel has demonstrated and lived our value and beliefs in practice through leadership and peer programs enabling them. My team knows far more about the quality of performance in daily practice and peer exchange. Thus, by placing trust with my employees to recognize excellence against the framework of what I express as service ideals and what we established as Values and Beliefs they can elicit reinforcing behaviors. My expectation is they will be empowered to make decisions that directly impact their employee experience as well as our customer experience.

Culture by Default

Culture by default is when a business builds a team and isolates the evaluation, selection and placement of talent to a business without culture in mind. Rather, the business looks at the person, their skills, and their abilities and overlooks the fact that their innate strengths are in fact going to be exhibited in the workplace as behaviors in commencement with many. Those behaviors are their values expressed in action. Thus, as we aim to build an empowered culture, perhaps an innovative culture, the question remains…How does each hire align their innate strengths into a culture while respecting who they are and the potential they bring to optimizing the team? I have included an organizational chart that expresses innate strengths and cognitive abilities of a team using BestWork DATA. Notice how each end of the spectrum is now identified not as behaviors but values. Personal values will be expressed in the workplace. How each diverse person and strength support overall culture is important to develop in the strategic culture plan. Without it, you get a culture topology like the sample I provide, where you need diversity but without an understanding of how that diversity benefits the team and the organization overall can lead to culture confusion and barriers to a high performing team.

Table 5.1   Sample Culture Topology Map

Lead With DATA

Experience is more valued		5	6	10	27	29	Fast learning is valued
Business-driven culture	7		20	14	4	1	Empathetic culture
Consensus seeking culture		2	3	14	46	9	Authoritative culture
Hesitates on change decisions		2	3	14	46	9	Decisive on change decisions
Flexible & adaptive culture		24	20	14	16		Rigid & defined culture
Innovative culture		24	20	14	16		Conservative & traditional culture
Competitive culture	3	37	13	15	5		Collaborative culture
Cool & impersonal culture		27	8	23	9	6	Warm & friendly culture
Empowering culture		2	3	14	46	9	Directive culture
Handles stress of change	9	17	20	23	5		Struggles with stress of change

Source: Russell, Charles. Feb. 2015. Reprinted with Permission.

The HRBoost Way

I share our organizational purpose (Vision, Mission, Service Ideals and Values) as a baseline of the Culture Invitation in my business. In Chapter 8, I have invited a number of larger and third party recognized employers that have successfully defined, created and built a culture that has been established and recognized as a winning workplace or employer of choice by a third party. This is unique to every business and in essence becomes the expressed Culture Invitation.

Our Vision: *We bring Joy and Purpose to people through their Work!*

This is the ideal and ultimately inspires me but ultimately each person that joins me on the journey to live the Vision. It is my why and it should be the why of anyone who joins the team at HRBoost.

Our Mission: *We offer services that allow your business to do what it does best. Helping companies contain costs, minimize employer related risk, and relieve the administrative burden of HR while creating results that rival big competition.*

This is the traditional WHAT, not the HOW!

Our Service Ideals

We are not responsive but rather we are proactive.
We aim to set the standard in service.
We believe presence is more than just being present.
We know transactional work meets transformational work.

These are the customer commitments we make to deliver brand promise. Essentially, these are deal breakers in service delivery.

Our Values and Beliefs

We are driven to overcome and achieve.
We live for life affirming work.
We choose to learn, evolve and grow.
We strive for collaborative strength.
We nurture well-being.
We help others and share for the benefit of all.
We commit to businesses who believe in the power of people.

These are beliefs linked to social, emotional, physical, spiritual, financial and family values that speak to personal and organizational frameworks allowing for my culture invitation to be expressed.

The Vision of my business is in reality our **Why?** We believe everyone deserves to find work that builds on their strengths and ties to a purpose they believe in. The **Why** should inspire you and the people that give their talents and graces to the business. Just imagine if everyone identified their innate strengths and aligned them to their work and their purpose. This is why we at HRBoost are inspired! Every day, we aim to help someone connect with their joy and purpose through their work.

The Culture Invitation presents a theory that has long been studied. That is that culture and leadership are on the same side of a two sided coin and as Edward Schein has studied, one cannot be clearly understood by itself[52]. Schein's work has clarified that culture is a complex group learning process that is only partially influenced by leadership behavior. It is important to note, leadership behavior is defined in the traditional sense of the word leadership vs. the definition I align to. I believe that everyone is a leader. Schein presents, however, that if a group's survival is threatened because culture elements have become maladapted, it is ultimately the function of leadership at all levels of the organization to recognize and do something about the situation. Schein presented that it is in this sense that leadership and culture are intertwined.

Redefining Culture

A business may find that they need to define the strategic culture plan and perhaps even their culture invitation years after a business was founded. I would argue in fact, that every business will need to establish a strategic culture plan and culture invitation that is forward thinking. Many may need to redefine or delve deeper into the meaning of their invitation as well as how it is expressed by leaders on the team today. Even if a business never defines the culture strategic plan or their culture invitation, their business most certainly has a formidable culture and often it is complete with sub cultures. The first step in facilitating transformation is identifying a baseline both qualitatively and quantitatively. A business cannot define where it would like to go without knowing where it is today. I see this most problematic in mergers and acquisitions whereby business is closed and culture is never a consideration. There are a number of workforce engagement surveys on the market today and careful consideration should be given to source a credible survey to purchase and/or participate in. Once aggregate data is reported, many businesses fail to share their results across the organization. If you are participating in a survey that does not provide aggregate or benchmark data, I would consider that a red flag. To survey and not share findings is damaging to a culture and can impact trust negatively as well as organizational credibility. If this is how an organization chooses to handle the "voice of the people," it is better off not asking for the "voice of the people." The aggregate data must be shared and then the organization must set forth what was heard and what will be done about it. If you happen to work for an organization that has not yet committed to culture strategically, then you must elect to be a leader that impacts positive change from wherever you lead from. I am one that believes that effective leaders can create positive retention despite the lack of a culture invitation. In fact, as a leader you can create positive change within your reach and it will show in your departmental results and metrics or even within your peer group. Unfortunately, it cannot reach across the organization without the leadership system across divisions. Working at this micro level on culture is not ideal as every leader should be identifying stakeholders and maximizing peer relationships across the organization and for the greater establishment of "we."

Dysfunctional Leadership

The reality is that not every work environment is led by leaders that fully embrace leadership as others would come to expect. In toxic environments, I have been one to witness incredible culture results despite what Dr. Ray Benedetto has expressed to me as "clinical dysfunctional leadership." In one of our first exchanges, he joked I was good at buffering around clinical dysfunctional leadership. I had never thought of my work in that way. I had to pause and think, have I witnessed dysfunctional leadership? What does it look like? A leader angry at work? Perhaps. Have I witnessed leaders who get outraged in frustration? Yes.

Have I seen one leader speak to another recalling from memory a relevant fact in presenting their case and the opposing leader puzzled and stating it was not at all true? Rather it was nonsense!? Yet, I was in that meeting too and in fact, it had been said and was true. Never had I framed it as clinical dysfunctional leadership. I have been fortunate to gain in knowledge from working with Dr. Ray Benedetto as a workforce alignment partner. In recent years it has become more definitive and Benedetto has set forth six factors that contribute to an environment that is, in fact, toxic and supportive of clinical dysfunctional leadership. Having worked in various business environments spanning twenty years, it becomes clear how widespread this problem can be. Consider the following examples[53]:

1   People in positions of leadership use power to force actions they prefer or believe right without considering the input of those who are closest to the situations the company faces;

2   Coercive and pace-setting leadership styles are visibly present, with narcissism, passive-aggressiveness, and other forms of negative control behaviors being prevalent;

3   Employees "hunker down" and simply try to get through the day-to-day activities to survive and earn their paycheck;

4   An aspirational organizational purpose that inspires all within the company to achieve their best is clearly absent;

5   Seniors within the company perceive front-line employees as dispensable, "plug and play" assets rather than the human capital upon which to build the enterprise;

6   Front-line leadership exhibits the trickle-down effects of poor senior leadership, where coercion and the threat of losing one's job are common tactics for getting results.

Many businesses monitor predictive (quantitative) factors without realizing or truly associating those factors to clinical dysfunctional leadership. Common factors I have discussed in a personal interview with Dr. Ray Benedetto, Co-Founder of GuideStar, Inc. include lost productivity that can be seen in high turnover, absenteeism, presenteeism paired with low morale within multiple departments with high error rates and/or rework. Another quantitative indicator is burdensome HR expenses for recruitment, employee relations and litigation response of which are tied to business asset protection and talent attraction vs. innovation or business growth.

Another quantitative indicator is the lack of quantitative date from the workforce itself. Cultural climate and employee surveys are rarely done, let alone valued in organizations whereby the voice of the people is projected as lip service rather than substantive change based on findings and root cause analysis.

Dr. Benedetto's research and work[54] has highlighted several cultural and normative (qualitative) factors that are also often associated with clinical dysfunctional leadership. First, one may realize they are working in a dominant "club" culture that is hard to penetrate with new talent from the outside. One example that comes to mind is when new leadership is acquired to help scale a business or take a high growth business to the next level. It can present when CEO/Founders have a hard time empowering the leaders they have placed to, in fact, enable the workforce. Often there is heavy reliance on management practices and a "Do as I say" mentality, which squashes individual creativity, initiative, positive change that leads to innovation and contribution to company growth. One of the most significant qualitative indicators in my opinion is what Benedetto cites as short-term extrinsic motivators like monetary incentives that are commonly used, further drawing on strained coffers. Lastly, on-going staff development is episodic, lacks continuity, and fails to account for the unique KASH (knowledge, abilities, skills, and habits) of a diverse and potentially positive workforce built with bench strength in mind.

The My Way Trap

I attended a session years ago that changed my outlook on what many in the psychological field would call clinical dysfunctional leadership[55]. To pretend that all of us have not witnessed troubling or even questionable human behavior in workplace environments would be remiss. I happen to be someone who believes in people regardless. I will share that back in 2008 I had a wonderful opportunity to attend a session that opened my eyes. I saw Dr. J.P. Pawliw-Fry present a session called, "The Epidemic of Playing Small: The My Way Trap." Dr. Pawliw-Fry is an internationally renowned thought leader on the subject of leadership, performance and managing under pressure[56]. He shared that there are many highly educated, skilled individuals who work in a wide variety of disciplines and industries. They have strong views about how work should be done and prefer a high degree of control in how they perform their jobs. These types of leaders need to be leaders of people, not projects. They may be just enough of an expert to lead, not do. He did a wonderful job of sharing that true leaders will have business competence but they must also embrace personal connection. He shared research from Blessing White on personal connection as a competency. Blessing White is a global consulting firm dedicated to Leadership Development and Employee Engagement. Cornerstone qualities of high performing leaders included Trustworthiness, Empathy, External Attunement and Depth. These are the qualities that matter and while I knew that even then, I did not truly understand the inner struggle of people to feel smart. He gave us insight into how the brain works and the physiological responses the brain and body employ in stress. If a person is raised to be smart, then to not be smart may feel like agony, even defeat. If the situation is judged as being stressful, the Hypothalamus (at the base of the brain) is activated. There is considerable variation in level and type of hormones released by different people and in response to different stressors. I walked away with a real understanding that the way a person's body responds to stress is quite simply not a simple physiological process. What I will never forget is that a person loses access to their short term memory in situations of high stress and this can last up to a few minutes. When I realized I had been witnessing this in meeting after meeting, it became clear; I was working with leaders that did not feel comfortable saying, "I don't know, please show me."

When building a culture that values leadership, leadership must be about not being the smartest or the best equipped but rather by being the person that is adept at learning, unlearning and re-learning. Reward team development and praise leadership behaviors that embrace adaptive learning. I walked away from that session with a great sense of compassion for every leader I have ever worked with and/or for. Clearly many are challenged by managing "smart" employees. Fundamental leadership questions as you consider leadership in another person, be it your leader, a stakeholder or a peer can be posed as, "What inspires you personally?" "What are you a leader for?" and "Why should anyone be led by you?"[57]. Some aspects of culture are buffered and there are various zones among teams and verticals of business. Results will vary and be significantly linked to the operational leadership in any respective division. I truly believe, however, that you can develop your skills as a leader and increase your value to an organization. Your presence can impact positive outcomes.

Preferably, your organization has committed to qualitative and quantitative data linked to leading indicators, values leadership at all levels, and created a process for upholding a strategic culture plan and the culture invitation as it is expressed day in and day out by leaders. Now that we understand leadership and culture are, in fact, intertwined, one must understand the theory of Organizational Leadership.

A Real Story: *AVMED, Inc.*

CEO: Michael Gallagher

AvMed's mission is to help their Members live healthier. They provide Members with quality, cost-effective plans, and excellent

Member services. As one of Florida's oldest and largest not-for-profit health plans, their corporate culture is defined by compassionate, collaborative and ethical behavior focused on delivering superior Member service. As a not-for-profit, they reinvest earnings to continually enhance services for Members.

In 2015, I had the pleasure of inviting Jennifer Blades to present at our Culture Leadership Summit. She shared an excellent story of a business that was already great but aimed to be even better. A true sign of an employer of choice is the commitment to continuous improvement. I have invited Jennifer to share her sentiments on the culture invitation. She actively works to integrate Generally Applied People Metrics, GAPM and Accountable Culture Management, ACM into their action planning and initiatives. The journey to excellence has taken a top down commitment that has inspired workforce integration to make a positive impact.

By Ms. Jennifer Blades, Director of Corporate Learning and Development, AvMed, Inc.

AvMed, Inc. is a not-for-profit community-based health plan operating in Florida and widely known for its exemplary member and provider satisfaction based on an industry leading commitment to service excellence. We are a great organization that realizes that everything we do internally reflects on us externally. Our internal service philosophy and standards, aligned with our organizational culture—from the way we make decisions—to how we serve each other—to how responsive we are—reinforces our external brand. The investment of intentionally promoting and building our desired culture never stops: it's a continuous cycle that's always evolving as the organization evolves. Both leaders and individual contributors play a critical role in developing and implementing our desired culture. Individual contributors provide important and insightful input on ways to continue growing and

106

developing the organization. Leaders lead the way by role modeling and demonstrating commitment to new norms. It's much easier to get buy-in when people feel like they have a say about what should change and see leaders' commitment and follow-through. We're now working to strengthen deep cross-functional relationships across the organization, improving line of sight to the big picture within a constantly changing industry, and optimizing our people practices to align to our desired culture. Our culture approach is to always "keep moving forward!"

The Culture Invitation is never enough. It must precede workforce alignment. AvMed, Inc. is living the invitation through workforce alignment and it embodies organizational leadership. However, in Chapter 6, we will explore organizational alignment within the context of **Organizational Leadership!**

CHAPTER SIX

Organizational Leadership

Leadership is among the most studied concepts today. To look back over the historical evolution of how leadership has been regarded, defined and enacted is beyond the scope of this chapter. Rather the intent is not to review the hundreds of definitions of what leadership is but rather present the concept of organizational leadership. We can begin with one complex definition of leadership that has evolved over the centuries. Effective leadership is defined as the interaction among members of a group that initiates and maintains improved expectations and the competence of the group to solve problems and attain goals[58]. Interestingly enough, this definition is not about headship, the individual, compliance or dominance. In fact, this definition incorporates "interaction" and "improved expectations" with respect to the "competence of the group" to "attain goals." It may well be one of the more evolved definitions I have discovered. Organizational leadership is about leadership throughout the organization and leadership is at all levels. Organizational leadership at the strategic level is how leaders develop culture.

We must begin with what we know. Efficiency is a construct that many businesses have become accustomed to and while it is not the opposite of innovation, the structure and behaviors that create either construct may be opposed. There must be a balance between efficiency and effectiveness but many businesses lean to efficiency. For years, I worked in manufacturing environments and the definition of success may very well have been viewed as cranking out as many widgets as possible. I actually have pondered who buys a million cans of brake cleaner! There was little thought given to work environment let alone well-being. I think back and honestly people could have well died from heat exhaustion. I remember Popsicle breaks as a safety protocol vs. for fun. Today, my clients are far more innovative and require a completely different set of behaviors that draws out the creativity from people. Businesses today require more than one mind to forge the future and compete.

Predating capitalism was evolution and regardless of your views, science presents reptiles and mammals. What does this have to do with organizational leadership you may ask? Well, the evolution of neurophysiology impacts every human at the most foundational level. Whether you are aware of this phenomenon or not, some part of you is constantly looking out for danger. Fear of the economy, your job, your financial situation, world terrorism. Whatever it may be your reptilian mind protects, while the mammalian mind connects. For your work to be meaningful, potentially innovative and even open to entertaining new ideas requires the environment in which you work must be perceptually safe. It makes sense to me as one cannot facilitate a meaningful retreat for a team without first addressing safety among those present. Not necessarily the safety of the room but the trust one imparts to another across the table. If the prehistoric part of you finds your environment to be unsafe it can compromise your ability to relate closely to people or work. The research of Stephen Porges, the former Director of the Brain-Body Center at the University of Illinois at Chicago has introduced the Polyvagal Theory[59]. His work has provided exciting new insights and refined our understanding into the way our autonomic nervous system unconsciously mediates social engagement, trust, and intimacy. The reality that we all must feel safe sequentially before being able to work together or explore new concepts is important. When we baseline organizational culture, we are aiming to identify the baseline for comparison to quantitative data later but also to determine the level of change needed to move from what some may call a reptile environment to a mammalian environment. In a reptile environment, you may feel profoundly alone. Imagine the furthest you will project is to whether you will survive the end of the day. Even highly driven quantitative environments that are metric driven can paralyze talent with fear of incompetence. If you are a reptilian leader, Porges argues you will take anything original that your direct reports do as volatility. In a mammalian habitat, the fact that we must work together is acknowledged. Porges presents that a mammalian environment will foster a consistent, stable, and secure environment with appropriate time and space to create. With the right mix, the talent can arise to the invitation of innovation in the form of bold thinking. There is no getting around the fact that people are humans. I love the way everything connects. From your engineering team to the culture invitation, if you want to get the best out of your team, perhaps even your entire workforce, then they need to feel invested in your vision and how it connects personally to their ability to make a positive contribution. As Faisal Hoque presented in his book the premise for the reptilian vs. mammalian environment[60] he stated so eloquently "You cannot tell a flower to grow, but you can provide the environment for it to bloom."

Given we are in fact humans; we cannot forget subconscious neurophysiology as we now consider capitalism as it relates to organizational leadership. The primary goal of a business in capitalism is to earn profits for the owners of the firm. Indeed many would argue the only reason that a business is formed is to earn profits for its owners. However, capitalism has long been corrupted by individual motives and greed. To be sustainable, it must serve more than stockholders and financial markets in the future. Drucker was among the first to declare that businesses cannot be defined or explained in terms of profit and in short, every organization is perfectly designed to achieve the results it gets[61]. Organizational leadership builds upon the premise of capitalism with intention to build great companies by driving profitability and sustainability through tenets and practices of shared leadership and character based capitalism. Breaking the mold from the simple definition of capitalism, the character-based capitalism is built to engage leaders at all levels, build organizational knowledge, align the workforce with organizational purpose and establish a character-based culture of performance excellence. At its core, organizational leadership is rooted in the term "character-based capitalism" to describe the beliefs, principles, and practices unique to the organizational leadership system for character-based capitalism[62]. The system itself has been built over the course of a decade and has been tested and proven within the middle market and municipal business environments where leaders were dedicated to building high performing organizations.

The Organizational Leadership System for Character-based Capitalism

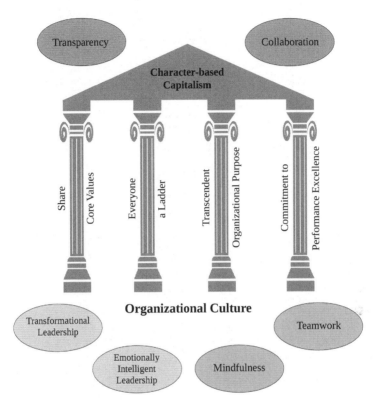

As you can see in the model, there are four pillars that foster continuous innovation and growth but the four pillars alone are not sufficient for building a culture of performance excellence. There are in fact a total of six attributes within a character-based organizational culture that must be built upon the four pillars and align with stages for organizational development. From Benedetto's foundational work on character-based culture, the authors of *It's My Company Too!* (Thompson, Benedetto, Walter, and Meyer) examined high performing, award winning organizations in several industries:

manufacturing, distribution, service, professional services, and construction, healthcare, and non-profit. From their research and continued work by Guidestar, Inc. co-founders, Benedetto and Fallek emerged the four pillars[63]:

Shared Core Values: These define the cultural foundation through which acceptable attitudes, behaviors, and practices are established, reinforced and rewarded;

Everyone within a Company is a Leader: Within a company everyone must be developed and appreciated as a leader because each has influence on decisions made by others, especially external customers who determine the economic value of the company;

Transcendent Organizational Purpose: A well-defined transcendent organizational purpose toward which everyone in the company gladly and willingly devotes mental and physical energies, not merely to make money but to make the world a better place; and

Commitment to Performance Excellence: Extending to and from everyone within the company because it drives continuous improvement and fosters collaboration, innovation and mindfulness.

The commitment to performance excellence depends on six key attributes through which leaders build the right culture for innovation and growth. Without these attributes, an organization cannot effectively align its workforce holistically. Dependent on the foundation of the four pillars the six attributes are as follows[64]:

Leadership: Understanding and applying the principles of emotionally intelligent and transformational leadership, essential to the character-based capitalism program. Both attributes depend on shared leadership, the development of leaders and their readiness to guide change and practice servant leadership;

Knowledge: Transparency throughout a company as well as collaboration (shared creation) are operating principles through which organizational learning can evolve;

Execution: Critical to execution is teamwork (vs. group work) and mindfulness through which individuals and teams innovate and perform better collectively.

In Chapter 5, the concept of entanglement vs. engagement was presented. Entanglement is the outcome of the alignment and execution of the six key attributes in conjunction with the four pillars, the foundation. Often, individuals must find ways to align themselves with the vision of an organization and they may not have the servant leaders at the helm. It is still possible to inspire and lead in an effort to bring meaning, joy, and purpose to the forefront. To know first then to be and lastly to lead is a three-step process coined as the *Inside-Out Effect*.[65] Through this method, every person can take a personal journey toward experiencing their work and life as a calling. They take you into the heart of greater fulfillment, performance, and leadership. To be truly mindful in your work is a personal journey working either in response to a culture invitation, a deeper calling or a journey to understanding and cultivating yourself. When you begin to live and lead in alignment with your authentic self, you embark on an incredible journey toward peak performance and peak happiness.

Appreciative Inquiry (AI) is a change management approach to a way of being and seeing. It is both a worldview and a process for facilitating positive change in human systems, e.g., organizations, groups, and communities. Its assumption is simple: Every human system has something that works right–things that give it life when it is vital, effective, and successful. AI begins by identifying this positive core and connecting to it in ways that heighten energy, sharpen vision, and inspire action for change. As AI consultant Bernard J. Mohr says,

"Problems get replaced with innovation as conversations increasingly shift toward uncovering the organization's (or group's, or community's) positive core[66]. "This is a proven process that can serve any leader well in working to bring shared leadership to the forefront. I have often had to work over a period of time to bring synergy to a leadership team gradually, allowing ideas and buy in to be exchanged organically. Culture is a process and creating a shared image of a preferred future is among the first achievements. Ironically, to walk into an organization that has the character-based capitalism framework would allow workforce alignment to take shape rapidly. It is the environment where all the tactical frameworks of roles, responsibilities, rewards and systems exist separate from the four pillars that prevent performance excellence from being lived. The framework of AI strives to enable powerful questions. Pose questions that are thought provoking and invite reflection, stimulate curiosity and help a team move forward through questions that begin with, "Why?" "What if?" "How?" Perhaps through your own positive inquiry you can spark the beginning of something that leads your organization to embrace organizational leadership vs. leadership ad hoc.

A Real Story: *Elk Grove Village*
Village Manager: Raymond R. Rummel

Elk Grove Village is a village located in northeastern Illinois adjacent to O'Hare International Airport and the city of Chicago. The village is located primarily in Cook County with a small portion in DuPage County.

It was not until I met a thought leader with a doctorate in Organizational Leadership that I realized the true opportunity available to every leader at the helm of business today. Dr. Ray Benedetto is an expert in organizational leadership. He is a retired US Air Force Colonel, a business owner and principal, a practitioner-scholar with a prominent MBA program, and an author, speaker, and talk radio contributor. I invited him to share a real story as his work in organizational leadership is creating real results. Not only for the private sector but the public sector as well.

By Dr. Ray Benedetto, Principal, GuideStar, Inc.®

The Financial Crisis of 2008 hit Elk Grove Village (IL) hard. Business relocations and closures reduced tax revenues, forcing depletion of cash reserves to offset budget deficits. Customer complaints, particularly with the building permit process, were increasing.

Municipal leaders were committed to fulfilling the vision of being **The Exceptional Community**, *but service excellence was far from a reality. A focus group with business leaders revealed they wanted working partnerships, reliable infrastructure services, and most of all lower taxes with fiscal responsibility. But several obstacles stood in the way of fulfilling these desires, not the least of which were municipal employees were more concerned with compliance and following rules while departments operated in functional silos. Not uncommon features of a government bureaucracy, but not at all acceptable if the Village was going to achieve its vision.*

Elk Grove leaders engaged GuideStar, Inc.® to facilitate an organizational transformation that would align all municipal employees, departments, and functions around four core values, the transcendent purpose of being the Exceptional Community, and the philosophy of Everyone Being a Leader because of the influence each was capable of exercising with internal and external customers. The multi-year transformation and the journey to performance excellence *continue to motivate and inspire Elk Grove Village employees. They have been able to (a) restore municipal reserves to pre-2009 levels, (b) provide better services such as a $13.6 million 2015 investment in infrastructure improvements, (c) gain 122 businesses in 2014 alone, (d) increase sales tax revenue by 20%, (e) cut corporate vacancy rates in half to 6%, and (f) achieve recognition as the best American city for establishing an international business (Global Trade Magazine), and the top town in Cook County (which includes Chicago), one of the top three cities within Illinois, and one of the top 10 in the US for locating a business. Municipal leaders credit GuideStar, Inc.® and the pervasive application of Character-based Capitalism tenets throughout Village operations as key contributors to the Village's success.*

Often, it takes just one to spark change. It goes back to change leadership vs. change management. I believe that it will take many conscientious leaders to invoke the change needed to address the Talent Emergency. If talent has won as I suggest, the intrapreneur is possibly one of the best competitive advantages a business can consider when contemplating how to entice the entrepreneurial spirit to stay within the traditional business and be fulfilled. A business must consider the leader, the intrapreneur within its grasp. I would propose that it was, in fact, a strong visionary leader and potentially an intrapreneur that brought GuideStar, Inc. to the Village of Elk Grove to facilitate a transformation. For this reason, we will explore **Intrapreneurship next!**

CHAPTER SEVEN

Intrapreneurship

Intrapreneurship is a fairly recent phenomenon sweeping the globe. If you were to peruse the web you would find a vibrant community open to exchange and support and dedicated to innovation within the businesses to which they dedicate themselves. Enough support exists to sustain an international conference, the 7th edition of which is in Munich, to promote Intrapreneurship since 2011. This year's theme happens to be "The Good, the Bad and the Ugly of Intrapreneurship." The concept of small, self-managing teams absent a hierarchy appears to be the intrigue of many a Fortune 500 employer. Yet, the term itself is derived and originates from the concept of Intrapreneuring, which Gifford Pinchot III presented in his first book, *Intrapreneuring: Why You Don't Have to Leave the Corporation to Become an Entrepreneur.* He expanded on the intrapreneurship concept and was noted in mainstream media as "stirring discussion within management."[67]

Pinchot presented in his original works that Intrapreneuring meant fundamentally two things[68]:

First, Intrapreneurship is a set of business practices that liberate people with entrepreneurial personalities to innovate rapidly inside larger organizations for the benefit of that organization and its customers. Second, an individual and/or a team act in an entrepreneurial manner to serve the best interests of the larger organization and its supply chain, with or without official support.

In recent years, the push of the Millennials, the need for global innovation, and the desire of skilled talent to do something new, different, and even meaningful has sparked new conversations around the concept of Intrapreneurship. Yet, the ROI of these programs is under scrutiny and not without challenges. In a published article by Fast Company, not all companies are embracing intrapreneurialism. Christie Smith, Deloitte's managing principal for consulting in the west region of the US, is an intrapreneur and now manages a team of them. She noted many reasons in a Fast Company article that not all companies are embracing intrapreneurship. One is that there are strong cultures of 'this is the way it's always been done.' There are also cultures that fear failure…or have very real reasons to be cautious. It can be right down to the personality of the leader itself.[69]

Sentiments like this drive Entrepreneurship vs. Intrapreneurship. If skilled and talented employees continue to feel ineffective, frustrated, and unable to achieve their goals, other opportunities will present themselves and businesses will net a talent loss versus a talent gain. Everyone deserves to find work that is built upon innate strengths and allows them to feel part of something greater than themselves. For Intrapreneurship to be effective I argue it must be supported by organizational leadership tenets. To compete against the external influence of freelance and entrepreneurial enterprise, businesses must change and adapt to create internal environments built for intrapreneurs.

Recall engagement and entanglement in Chapter 3. The key difference between an engaged employee and one who is entangled is engaged employees work individually with inconsistent results throughout an organization. Thus, engagement is insufficient for achieving overall organizational success. Entangled employees connect to organizational purpose and use their discretionary efforts, being both individual time and energy, to solve organizational challenges[70]. The culture invitation ensures that every person has the opportunity to be entangled, to think and act like owners. Intrapreneurs who are not working organizationally but rather departmentally or individually will, in fact, be optimally engaged rather than entangled.

To understand the concept of *Everyone is a Leader*, one of the four pillars presented in the Organizational Leadership system from Chapter 6, it is important to review the different roles among all leadership levels in an organization. Jim Collins[71] defined five levels of leadership within organizations, but the five levels spin three distinct roles of leadership that build culture and enable workforce alignment: Strategic, Operational and Grassroots[72].

Levels of Leaders

Copyright 2008-2016 by GuideStar, Inc. ®

Strategic Leadership (Levels 4 and 5) looks outward and must be especially sensitive to the external environment and organizational awareness. Defining and protecting organizational purpose as well as culture is paramount at this level along with governance. Recognition systems, strategic decision making and problem solving, and ongoing knowledge creation, which are the root of innovation and change, fall within the purview of strategic leaders.

Operational Leadership (Level 3) aligns organizational structures with organizational purpose to execute necessary actions for the achievement of strategic goals. Operational leaders bear overall responsibility for selecting the right people for the right jobs and establishing policies and procedures to execute the processes that achieve goals. Making good, ethical decisions, establishing and implementing performance management and reward systems, and ensuring knowledge management systems are in place to support information based decisions all fall within the purview of operational leadership.

Front Line Leadership (Level 1 and 2), also known as Grassroots Leadership, must demonstrate integrity while willingly contributing and sharing ideas that can improve individual and unit performance. Connecting personal actions to organizational purpose and culture (vision, mission, and values) is critical in executing tasks with a strong commitment to service excellence. Level 2 leaders encourage others to share ideas and create harmony by showing care and trust, the foundational values of lasting relationships. In the essence of teamwork and shared leadership, these leaders help others achieve their goals and foster good communication by exercising presence and listening to others.

How Leadership Levels Build the Culture of Character

Level 5 Leadership	Strategic Leadership	Defining, Creating, and Building the Culture of Character	Hire for Character; Put Right People in the Right Seats
Level 4 Leadership			
Level 3 Leadership	Operational Leadership	Modeling and Reinforcing the Culture of Character	
Level 2 Leadership	Grass-roots Leadership	Learning and Living the Culture of Character	Select Self In or Out of Culture
Level 1 Leadership			

Copyright 2008-2016 by GuideStar, Inc.®

When leaders build culture around all levels of leadership, develop managers as leaders vs. managers, enact change leadership vs. change management with a clear line of sight to organizational purpose, and foster transparency and collaboration, virtually any level leader within a business can be an intrapreneur. With the ability to exercise teamwork and mindfulness for the benefit of all stakeholders, the commitment to performance excellence can be realized and only then can a high performing organization be achieved. The model above demonstrates how it takes all levels of leaders working in synergy to build a character based culture.

Strategic Leadership (Levels 4 and 5) defines and creates the culture invitation that in fact is the foundation. It must link to the vision and mission but also express the inherent intrinsic organizational purpose.

Operational Leadership (Level 3) is responsible to model the behavior, leading by example and acting as coaches in a servant leadership style. As they model, they reinforce the culture with systems and rewards that keep silos at bay, empowering individuals as leaders themselves.

Front Line Leadership (Level 1 and 2) must be willing to identify the culture invitation and verify that in fact their personal values align to the organizational values of the organization. They then can learn to live the values through their behaviors in everything they do, thus living the culture of character. When this occurs, peer accountability can take place within every corner of a business as it is not top down. In contrast, when every leader upholds the values, the culture is supported by peer accountability. Self deselection can take place quickly in an organization that is in fact living their culture when an individual leader finds their personal values are not in alignment with organizational values.

Towers Perrin conducted a Global Workforce Study[73] of more than 90,000 employees in 2008. Even then, during the recession and troubling economic times, there were leaders in business strategically focused on maintaining a servant leadership model. Those businesses that achieved and/or maintained an employer of choice endorsement were not solely focused on profit. They lived the model of leading businesses in the interest of every stakeholder. Despite pay freezes, layoffs, and dwindling profitability there were businesses that learned a great deal about people. It is a survey from an interesting moment in time and though it was years ago, what employees need from their employers to feel engaged and motivated has not changed. This is critical to point out. What leaders needed to do then and now remains the same. They uncovered the top 10 items that drive employee engagement around the world and highlighted them as follows:

Senior management's sincere interest in employee well-being.
Opportunities for employees to improve skills and capabilities.

The organization's reputation for social responsibility.
Opportunities for employees to have input in their departments'
decision making.
The organization's ability to quickly resolve customer concerns.
An employee's readiness to set high personal standards.
Excellent career advancement opportunities.
An employee's interest in challenging work assignments.
An individual's relationship with his or her supervisor.
The organization's encouragement of innovative thinking.

A Real Story: *An Intrapreneur*

I met Jamie when I was consulting to a high growth business in a high tech industry. He was hired at a sensitive time when the business sought ambitious and capable individuals to hit the ground running. I had the pleasure of witnessing Jamie take on challenges. Most significant was the way he created a role for himself. Most will seek the traditional career path for opportunity but Jamie created a role that was not present, developed the vision of the business opportunity, created buy-in at the executive level and ultimately support. I invited him to share his story from his view. May his perspective inspire leaders to see the key exchange that inspired him to lead.

By: Mr. Jamie Lutkus, Senior Engineering Manager, Research and Development

Almost five years ago my wife and I made a decision to move to the Midwest in order to be closer to our families. This life change also presented an opportunity to really look for the best type of company that would support the professional challenges I was looking for. I had spent the previous five and a half years with a large defense contractor. During that period, our customer had spent a large amount of time looking for ways to force our company to look at our work differently, but most were fought with resistance. I found this time period frustrating because there were many opportunities to implement improvements and reduce the operating cost of the contract, which might have reduced our revenue. In fact, it would have also opened new opportunities. I knew based off this experience that I wanted to find an organization which supported creative thinking and new ideas.

When I arrived at the new company it was a small but very quickly growing company. It didn't take long for opportunity to present itself. On the first day I arrived, the company had an immediate need for the formation of a group with a very niche technical capability. I was asked by the company owner to form a group that looked at the problem from an entirely different perspective. He encouraged me to form the group not as others have, but instead to create it as if it was my business and I needed to create a capability that discriminated us from other groups. Those words resonated with me at a very deep level. It caused me to take a risk and agree to the challenge. I had the responsibility to create something that had value, but how I got there was entirely up to me. I worked as if I were the business owner and the leadership of the company were my investors. Due to this experience I am now always looking for opportunities which can be created within my organization which result in company growth. When you're with an organization motivated to promote this type of thinking, it can result in growth for both parties.

Stories like Jamie's remind us that anyone can be an intrapreneur. It is people like Jamie that can make an impact on a business thriving through innovation. The fact is that we must remember there were businesses leading then. Many were being recognized not once, not twice but in some cases a decade consecutively. It is these businesses that have built a culture that lives and sustains. I have invited them to share their culture invitations and results with you in Chapter 8. Let's take a closer look at some of the best of the best out there in **Strategies from the Best of the Best and Brightest!**

CHAPTER EIGHT

Strategies & Dividends from a Few of the Best

What does it mean to be an employer of choice? Through my years of experience with Best and Brightest Companies to Work For™ I would venture to say winning organizations strive to not only make their companies better but they strive to make the lives of their employees better. Recognized employers seek valuable credible data to stay ahead of the competition but most important they value the talent that brings their vision to light. It is never about what the company says about themselves but rather what the people say about their employer that resonates. Third party award programs that only take employer surveys are not taking the voice of the people into their findings. Winners often share best practices to stay inspired and innovative and each knows that the investment in people returns on the bottom line. It is more than a marketing initiative or HR Excellence. It is truly about people coming together to enrich one another, engage a community and bring meaning not only to their work but to their sense of accomplishment through their work. Every business has a story. I have had the pleasure of touring and meeting with leaders of winning organizations throughout Chicago for over a decade. In this chapter I have invited a few of the best employers I have come to know to share their strategies and results. May their culture invitations, shared values and proven ROI in accolades inspire you to lead from wherever you may be.

Furthermore, I have asked each to share the challenges they are facing in the coming five years. Even the best are strategically planning for the future and often people misunderstand the best to be about perks and bonus programs alone. May it be known that in reality, businesses that are recognized are strategically sharing their visions with their talent today knowing all can partner now to WIN together in the future. Many still ponder what the leading indicators are when it comes to measuring the ROI of engagement. Few know engagement is only one of the five leading indicators revealed in a study conducted by The Human Capital Institute (HCI) and PS Culture Matters. The two partnered to conduct this research to gain a deeper understanding about how building and sustaining a performance culture impacts business productivity and financial performance. This research profiles exactly how culture manifests in organizations through the use of 11 key culture metrics, and provides a more comprehensive perspective on what metrics are most important for organizations to capitalize on in order to reap increased financial and performance benefits[74]. The most significant finding from their research study is that there are ultimately five key culture metrics that drive 14% to 17% higher financial performance in business. Thus, they are leading indicators not lagging indicators. Every business should have a pulse and quantitatively be measuring these five culture metrics. While all metrics tied to culture can drive value, it is certainly enlightening to know those that specifically correlate to financial performance. The study revealed them as:

Collaboration
Employee Engagement
Job Satisfaction
Professional Growth and Development
Alignment with Organizational Values

The study proposed in closing that some organizations are doing more to create a culture by design vs. by default. However, the trend in proactively creating a performance culture that drives business impact appears to be growing. That was in 2013. I only can hope it becomes a trend that revolutionizes businesses of all size and industry. Given my experiences in the middle market, I have yet to be convinced that the vast majority of businesses are ready for *The Talent Emergency*. The journey can take years and for those that have yet to express their vision and culture invitation in a meaningful and authentic way, may this book inspire you to begin the journey. Better yet, I invite you to lead the journey and perhaps be another who champions the journey.

A Real Employer Of Choice: *The Assurance Agency*
CEO: Mr. Anthony Chimino
By Mr. Steven Handmaker, Chief Marketing Officer

Steven is a self-described Brand Strategist, Engagement Evangelist and often speaks publicly about workplace culture, employee engagement and the ROI of an Engaged Workforce.

When Assurance began its quest to be recognized as a Great Place to Work, calculating the ROI admittedly wasn't top of mind. The company was simply trying to shift its operation into growth mode, and recognized employee engagement wasn't where it needed to be. Hence, it developed a core principle that "Happy Employees = Happy Clients." The basic idea was that if Assurance employees were happy and engaged in the work they were doing, it would translate into more satisfied clients who would in turn, do more business with us and refer us to other potential clients.

As part of this working ideology, it became very important to define what it meant to be a happy and engaged employee. As we saw it, an engaged employee:

- *Enjoys the place they work*

- *Enjoys the job they do*

- *Is proud to tell people about their employer*

- *Has a desire to help their employer improve*

- *Has a career goal and a plan to get there*

- *Knows where to internally get help*

- *Knows what their company does or makes*

132

- *Knows how their job impacts a customer*

- *Knows how all areas of the company impacts customers*

With these definitions firmly rooted and agreed upon, we set out to line up our business practices to ensure we were making each of these statements a reality for Assurance. Soon, our efforts began to bear fruit, and business began to soar. With daily reminders of the power of this employee-focused strategy, we've spent years honing and cultivating our culture to live up to these ideals and we've been rewarded each year with local, national and industry specific recognition as a Great Place to Work.

Calculating the specific Return on Investment for the strategy as a whole is kind of like trying to decide just how important an engine is to a car's success. Still, there are many specific dollars we can directly account for. For example, Assurance has taken a leadership stance as to the power of wellness and consumerism in lowering medical benefit expenses. We've asked a lot from our employees to go on this journey with us, and it's only through their engagement with Assurance and commitment to our mission, that we've achieved the level of success we have. Since 2004, the average increase per employee, per year, for medical benefits is 13.4%. At Assurance, our average increase over the same period is 3.5%. The savings to Assurance is nearly $10M.

Apart from our medical benefits, when compared to our peers, we have lower than average turnover, recruiting expenses, and sick days taken. At the same time, we experience higher than average client retention, employee tenure, employee referrals and overall revenue per employee.

Our Company

Assurance is one of the largest and most awarded independent insurance brokerages in the U.S. We provide personalized, expert advice and support in the areas of business and personal insurance, employee and executive benefits, surety bond placement, safety consulting, claims advocacy, retirement advisory services and strategic wellness programs. To serve the needs of our clients, Assurance contracts with the top insurance carriers in the country to deliver the widest breadth of options available.

Our Vision

Our long term vision is to one day credibly calculate that we create $1 billion in value annually for our clients.

Our Purpose and Why

The work we do on behalf of our clients allows every Assurance employee the opportunity to makes a huge impact on the world. Everyone here, every day, is driven by the chance to:

> Improve the quality of people's lives
> Help workers avoid injury, even save lives
> Help families gain access to needed medical care
> Make a secure and comfortable retirement possible for millions
> Grow the economy and increase the number of employable jobs
> Increase happiness in the workplace and society in general

Our Mission

Our mission is to minimize risk and maximize health.

Our Service Ideals

We firmly believe happy employees equal happy clients. In fact, our culture and success are founded on it. We go above and beyond to treat our greatest assets (our employees) well because stellar client service starts with them.

Our Shared Values and Beliefs

While many other companies often have a long list of core values, we don't – we have something way better. We decided the longer the list of 'core values' the harder it is for employees to remember and for leadership to reinforce. We've had great success with our simplified version: the Assurance D.N.A., which stands for "Dominate. Navigate. Appreciate."

*We **dominate** the competition with the greatest sales, service and operational staff in the industry. We **navigate** our clients through the intricacies of the insurance world. And we **appreciate** our 'A' off – for employees and clients alike, from annual celebrations to daily high-fives, recognition and handwritten notes.*

Our Dividends and Accolades/ROI

As an insurance brokerage, we know first-hand the value of engaged employees: they're more productive, more profitable, less likely to be involved in accidents, less prone to absenteeism, less likely to leave the company, better at engaging customers and more. Since 2004, for example, we've seen a 24:1 return-on-investment from our wellness efforts, a feat that couldn't happen without employee engagement.

Hiring and keeping TOP talent.

Our culture has not only directly and positively affected our bottom line and made recruiting and employee retention a breeze, it's helped us win business. We're our own best case study and we can prove it. While the cost of medical benefits are skyrocketing for companies around the country, our year-over-year increases are a fraction of the national average, thanks to engaged employees whom we guide to live well and make wise benefit choices.

Our perception of the greatest challenge facing businesses in the coming five years

Employee engagement has been the bedrock of our own success so we know its value. In the coming years, businesses the world over are going to be challenged like never before to maintain high levels of employee engagement as multi-generational workforces combine with increasing decentralization of traditional office locations. The shift to work-anywhere approaches while promoting greater flexibility and a decrease in real estate expenses for companies, will require even greater efforts to maintain employee engagement in order to best serve the customer, and the company as a whole.

A Real Employer Of Choice: *Brilliant*™
CEO: Mr. Jim Wong
By Mr. Jim Wong

Jim founded Brilliant in 2009. Brilliant is a search, staffing and management resources firm specializing in accounting, finance and information technology. The firm represents high-quality professionals and hiring companies in the greater Chicago and south Florida markets.

The Brilliant name and logo come from the Chinese translation for the sun and moon – and when combined – create a heightened awareness, or a brilliant state of mind. The firm's expert team uses that awareness to match companies with top talent in the industry. Brilliant represents high-quality accounting, finance and IT professionals, and companies within the manufacturing, distribution, health care, professional services, retail, and nonprofit industries, among many others.

Our Company

Founded in 2009, Brilliant™ is an award-winning search, staffing and management resources firm specializing in the accounting, finance and IT professions. The firm's team of business development and recruiting experts include former Big 4 CPAs, former hiring managers and other leading, industry professionals in the greater Chicago and south Florida markets.

Our Vision

Our Vision is to the leader in every business, niche and market that we serve.

137

Our Purpose and Why

See our mission.

Our Mission

Our mission is simple: To make people's lives better and that includes our clients, candidates and colleagues.

Our Service Ideals

Whether someone is looking to hire or looking to get hired, Brilliant is there as a resource for the accounting, finance and IT professions.

We represent high-quality accounting, finance and IT professionals in the greater Chicago and south Florida labor markets—and work diligently with our client companies to find the best fit for all—so that everyone can achieve success!

We guide our clients through every step of the hiring process, which reduces risk, lowers costs, and compresses their timeline so that we can have the right talent in the organization as soon as possible. Alternatively, we guide our candidates through every step of the job-search process from resume building to interviewing to accepting the job offer.

*We take a consultative approach and meet with our clients and candidates on a one-on-one basis to get a full understanding of expectations and goals. We offer management and hiring advice—so that our clients know what to look for and expect out of our job candidates applying for their roles. We provide useful tools and data to support our recommendations. And most importantly, we also stay on top of industry **trends**, emerging regulations and other important information affecting the accounting, finance and IT professions.*

We save our clients time and money by thoroughly evaluating, screening and testing our candidates. We know the right questions to ask in order to assess their skill level and knowledge. We then perform reference and background checks on each individual to confirm their experience and abilities. In addition, we verify education, degrees and certifications, and offer skills-assessment testing. Since our technical experience allows us to be so efficient in our screening, we are able to spend time evaluating candidates' **soft skills**, as well. As a result, our candidates can hit the ground running and are able to fit in the company's culture immediately.

We offer our temporary and contract employees full health benefits including medical, dental and vision as well as 401k options. We also provide vacation and holiday pay.

Our Shared Values and Beliefs: Brilliant is dedicated to upholding the highest of standards. We have six core values that we incorporate into our day-to-day culture and look for in our team members. Those values include Integrity, Job Satisfaction, Service, Accountability, Entrepreneurship and Teamwork.

Our Dividends and Accolades/ROI

Since its inception, Brilliant has made impressive strides in growth and success—emerging as a leader within the staffing and recruiting industry. As a result, Brilliant has been recognized with the following awards and achievements:

Inavero's 2016 Best of Staffing® Talent Satisfaction

No. 1 fastest-growing company on 2015 Crain's Chicago Business Fast 50

One of the fastest-growing private companies in America on 2015 Inc. 5000

No. 2 on 2015 Staffing Industry Analysts Fastest-Growing Staffing Firms

Chicago's Best and Brightest Companies to Work For® in 2014, 2015

Nation's Best and Brightest Companies to Work For® in 2014, 2015

Most recently, Brilliant CEO Jim Wong, CPA (Inactive) was recognized on the Staffing 100 List 2016 for North America as one of the most influential people in the industry.

Our perception of the greatest challenge facing businesses in the coming five years

The biggest challenge we see facing businesses in the coming years will be the war for talent. Innovation is disrupting every industry. As a result, it will force businesses to be more competitive. More than ever businesses will need to create value for all of their stakeholders. The companies with the best talent will have the best chances of succeeding. - Jim Wong, CPA (Inactive), CEO, Brilliant™

A Real Employer Of Choice:
Integrated Project Management (IPM)
CEO: Mr. C. Richard Panico
By Ms. JoAnn T. Jackson, Vision Realization Officer

Jo Jackson currently serves as IPM's Vision Realization Officer, a position she assumed in 2015, and previously served as Chief Financial Officer since IPM's inception in 1988.

Our Company

Integrated Project Management Company, Inc. (IPM) was founded in 1988 when project management was scarcely understood, much less considered a profession. Our founder and CEO, C. Richard Panico (Rich) recognized that many companies struggled due to inefficiencies and an inability to reliably execute critical initiatives. This observation led to the business rationale for a company whose core competency would be professional project management. We would help others get things done!

Our Purpose and Why

"IPM's essential purpose is to provide exceptional project leadership." This is the first sentence of Our Mission & Beliefs and it tells the world what to expect from IPM. But why?

*Good ideas, innovations, best intentions – these are all valuable, but if they cannot be translated into results, stagnation will set in. If they **can** be translated into results, everybody wins. IPM provides exceptional project leadership so that everybody can win.*

"Everybody" certainly includes our clients as we lead their projects to successful conclusions, but just as important, we feel a responsibility for our employees to win. That means they feel challenged, respected, cherished. They have opportunities to learn and to laugh; to create and to critique; to grow and to give. When they can apply their talents, feel the satisfaction of success, and retain energy and time for their families and the community at large, everybody wins.

"Everybody" also includes the cities where we have offices and where our employees live, the economic engines that fuel democracy, and the country in which we are based. Exceptional project leadership can improve the competitiveness of a company, the viability of a community, and the freedom of a nation.

That's why.

Our Fundamental Values, Our Mission & Beliefs, and Our Vision

At the point where a company exists only on a piece of paper as a business plan, that's the best time to establish the company culture. Clearly articulating the key behaviors which are absolute requirements of success within an organization – and then living and reinforcing them day in and day out – that's how a culture is established. Of paramount importance from day one at IPM was that the Company would be based on honesty, integrity, and ethical precepts. These precepts have guided every business transaction and catalyzed the extraordinary culture of top performers for which IPM is known. More recently, these precepts have been laid out clearly as our Fundamental Values.

Our Fundamental Values

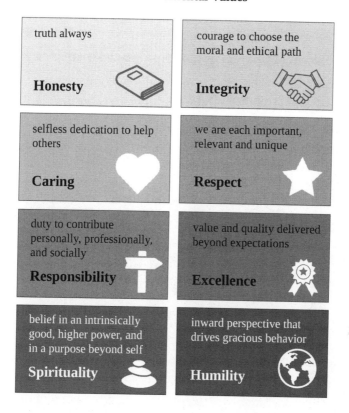

These Values, of which spirituality forms the foundational piece, have always been intertwined in **Our Mission & Beliefs** – a document too long to show here in its entirety, and too important to shorten. Suffice it to say, it is the governing document of the IPM's conduct, decisions, and strategy as they relate to our employees and clients; and the conduct expected of our employees as it relates to the Company, fellow employees, and our clients. The last paragraph of Our Mission & Beliefs succinctly captures the realization of our mission: IPM's Mission is honored each time a client's expectations are exceeded, each time an employee achieves his or her dreams, each time IPM earns an employee's loyalty, and each time the

Company's efforts positively influence our society and the world in which we live.

If Our Fundamental Values delineate core principles of behavior and Our Mission & Beliefs expound on actions taken, then Our Vision articulates the results of these actions. It clearly states how we will be perceived by our clients, while enabling our employees to see the extraordinary opportunities that will be afforded them.

Our Vision

IPM will be the global leader in project management-centric business consulting, renowned for our ability to resolve complex problems, execute major initiatives, and enable progressive organizational change and adaptability. IPM's passion is a sustained existence...to our centennial and beyond. Our reputation will be synonymous with excellence, ethical and insightful leadership, community involvement, and the highest commitment to the well-being of our family members.

To add clarity to Our Vision, five Vision Priorities were identified and elaborated upon:

Our Vision Priorities	
Global Market Leadership	Impeccable reputation and global brand recognition Leaders in our chosen markets Catalyst for ethical conduct Innovative mindset
Growth	Entrepreneurial spirit Ever-increasing size, customer base, and influence Many offices, services, and markets Sustainable and organic

Stability, security, longevity, and strength

Financial rewards

Pride of association

Peace of mind

Extraordinary culture which embodies Our Mission & Beliefs

Challenging and rewarding career

Renowned employee training and development

Personal satisfaction and engagement

Good neighbor and civic leader

Influencer in upgrading the quality of education

Contributor to the betterment of society and the well-being of children

These five Vision Priorities are somewhat immutable and no specific timeframe is identified. However, their specific shape will morph over time as goals are reached, milestones surpassed, or external factors reflected. To add clarity to elements of Our Vision that are within grasp in a shorter timeframe, the Vision 2020 Goals were established in 2010. These goals addressed these topics:

Recognition

Market reach

Revenue dollars and diversity.

Number of employees

Profit and rewards

Culture

Employee opportunity and engagement

Philanthropic goals

All of our strategic and continuous improvement efforts ultimately are captured in Annual Plan Initiatives so that all of our employees *know specifically how we plan to progress and how they can be of assistance to influence IPM's future. We report on all of these items when we meet – the entire company gathers four times each year. These meetings, perhaps better than anything else, prove how much the Company cares about employees connecting to each other. Our full day quarterly Staff Meetings include business topics to be sure, but a great portion of the time is reserved for social interaction. Laughs go a long way to build friendships and connection!*

Our Service Ideals

The highest possible value.

When clients engage our services, they should always be "Wowed." The services we provide should amaze and delight – both in the tangible results and in ROI.

IPM has learned that process, discipline, and leadership are the key ingredients for delivering that value. We are committed to our core competency – project planning and execution – and this enables excellence. We proactively measure the benefits of this excellence to ensure that our clients consistently realize a significant return on their investment.

And we also focus to ensure that the results our clients receive are sustainable after we have left the building. This focus requires more than understanding the technical and business requirements of any project. It requires a thorough understanding of the values, philosophies, and cultural markers that define an organization's DNA. We not only care about and nurture the culture at IPM, we uncover and influence, to the greatest extent possible, the culture of our clients. We can only accomplish these ideals if we employ extraordinary people.

It starts with a recruiting process that ends with employment of a select few. The process is rigorous: the number of IPMers that an applicant interacts with is minimally eight and frequently double digits. We are transparent about who we are and what we require. (Even the gentleman who serves our applicants by driving them from the airport to our office has a clear understanding of our requirements!) We welcome people to join us if we have concluded that they have the values and skills required, but we remind them that they are joining us, we are not joining them. This is not to appear arrogant or myopic, but to honor those already in our ranks who have every right to expect that we will continue to grow with colleagues who also value those ideals which drew them to IPM.

Then IPM invests significantly in training and development, typically averaging more training hours per year per employee than most Fortune 500 companies. But there is hugely important training that would never be coded on a timesheet as such. This is the training that occurs when an employee faces an issue and reaches out to ask a colleague for assistance. Unselfish, helpful, generous, collaborative – these are words that IPMers repeatedly use to describe their peers.

This section would be incomplete without mentioning how important "service" is to our employees and hence our culture. IPM's philanthropic activities fall under a program called "Project Mercy." While kindness and compassion have always been apparent at IPM, it took the brainchild of one of our corporate staff members to develop and propose a program that enables all employees across the country to join in support of a particular cause each quarter. Employees volunteer their time and talent, and both the Company and the employees open their wallets to help the less fortunate – in health, wealth, or spirit. This is truly service.

Service ideals would remain ideals were it not for the IPM family members who make them reality.

Our Dividends and Accolades/ROI

When IPM's management sought outside validation for our claim of a culture focused to ethics and integrity, and an environment that truly cares about its people, here is what resulted:

2004 – Chicago Better Business Bureau's Torch Award for Marketplace Ethics

2005 – Council of BBB International Torch Award for Marketplace Ethics

2008 – "Top Small Workplace" by Winning Workplaces and the Wall Street Journal

2009 - Chicago Better Business Bureau's Torch Award for Marketplace Ethics

2010 – Honorable Mention – Council of BBB International Torch award

2010 – American Business Ethics Award by the Financial Services Professional Foundation

2015 – Association of Management Consulting Firms "Spotlight Award" for Customer Engagement

2015 – Crain's Chicago "Top Small Workplace for Millennials"

2016 – One of 25 companies named "America's Best Small Businesses" by Forbes Magazine

2016 – One of 20 consulting firms named to SPI Research's 2016 "Best-of-the-Best" list

And

2010, 2011, 2012, 2013, 2014, 2015 - "Best Small Workplace" by Great Place to Work Institute® and Fortune Magazine

Our perception of the greatest challenge facing businesses in the coming five years

Work is part of life. The greatest challenges facing businesses are the same as those facing people in general. How can we grow as individuals, influence positive change through our work, take care of ourselves and our families, do well by doing good, embrace diversity while respecting convention, open our minds to new ideas while preserving as appropriate that which has made us successful to date, honor each other as individuals with unique skills while pushing each other to continually improve, earn accolades without making these the goal.

IPM is not driven by phenomenal profits (though we strive to make good business decisions) or extravagant growth (though we want to consistently offer opportunities). We are driven to be the best (acknowledging we will always be imperfect). Our greatest challenges in the next five years will be the same as they have been since 1988:

Finding outstanding, talented, dedicated, loyal, bright, hard-working, fun-loving people to join our quest to provide amazing value to our clients.

Securing work with clients who share our values, acknowledge our differentiation, and care about our success.

A Real Employer Of Choice: *The Pepper Group*
CEO & Founder: Mr. Tim Padgett
By Mr. Tim Padgett

In 1994, Tim Padgett set out to create a new marketing services company. One that would provide clients with the utmost quality and value, and provide employees with a great place to work, learn and grow.

Our Company

The Pepper Group is a recognized Marketing communications firm, specializing in B2B middle market and Fortune 500 companies. In addition to marketing-focused strategic and design services, Pepper Group also has a suite of HR Communication services. We help companies with their recruiting and employee retention initiatives through outstanding communications.

Teer1 is a Premier Employee Volunteering Program. Teer1 provides consulting, a methodology, and software for companies to run their programs.

Our Purpose and Why

Pepper Group—We Move People. Everything we do is intended to move our clients' audiences in the directions that they want them to move. This can be through education, humor, a challenging of biases or perspectives, etc. Likewise with sales performance—moving it higher. We also move our employees to greater heights in their careers.

Teer1—To facilitate more volunteering, specifically utilizing the vast wealth of human capital within the companies of America and internationally.

150

Our Shared Values and Beliefs

Initiative Has No Boundaries

Take personal responsibility to make whatever you do the best it can be. If you see an opportunity, jump on it yourself or get some help. Look at things differently—the solution may be hidden.

Work and Play with Passion

Communicate your passion and excite clients. Play hard so that you have great life experiences to draw from.

Pride in Craft and Service

Realize that it's a pretty cool business that we're in. Yin and Yang—the fun we have has another side and we need to do the hard things with equal verve.

Instead of a client-driven relationship, remember that we play an equal, valuable role, for which we are rewarded—monetarily and with a unique sense of accomplishment. When in doubt, kill 'em with kindness.

Strength of the Wolf is in the Pack

Support each other. Teach each other. Protect each other. Respect each other. Surprise each other. Cover each other's sixes.

Be Smarter Tomorrow

Our advantage as a company and as individuals is in our education and the skill sets we bring to the table. Pursue knowledge like it was gold and it will be.

Scraped Knees Teach Us to Dance

Don't be afraid to fall down. Pick yourself up, learn, and try again. You'll learn to run—maybe even fly.

Face to Face with Grace

When you can, be there in person. When you can't, be there on the phone. When you have to, communicate through email. Conversations are more efficient and personal when you look someone in the eye. They can feel your passion.

Choose to be Challenged

Wake up in the morning with a confident attitude and ride it through the day. Expect the unexpected. Explore your limits and help others do so, too. Be brave—what's the worst that can happen?

Our Dividends and Accolades/ROI

Pepper Group has been recognized as one of the 101 Best & Brightest Companies to Work For™ in Chicago in 2013, 2014 and 2015 and a Best Place to Work in Illinois™ in 2015.

We have also been recognized by B-to-B Magazine as a Top Agency for six consecutive years.

In 2015 we were included in the Inc5000.

It shows in our work product, winning many design awards from Graphic Design USA, the Business Marketing Association and the American Marketing Association.

Our perception of the greatest challenge facing businesses in the coming five years

The need to continuing to innovate at a pace that stays ahead of the start-up. The cost to be a start-up, in all but the most equipment-heavy industries, is so small. They can disrupt an industry in a heartbeat and established companies, though asset rich, will have to find ways to fight tradition and be nimble.

Although each generation has always moved "faster" than the one before it, never before have we seen escalation be so prevalent.

With these things in mind, it will take our bodies a while to catch up. Thousands of years of evolution have made our bio systems work the way they do. Only in the last 100 years have we been accelerating our life pace at a phenomenal level.

Businesses will have to encourage employees to utilize practices that bring their bodies, and minds, into a sustainable rhythm. Practice yoga, meditation, and the arts. These are things that naturally readjust a person's biometric balance.

Businesses cannot ignore this phenomenon and still have sustainable innovation without burning people out in short timeframes. There is much to gain from employees who stick around and survive the cycles that businesses must endure to thrive for long periods. If unicorns (and their smaller cousins) become the norm for business models, there will societal impact. What that will be is still unknown to most of us.

A Real Employer Of Choice: *Radio Flyer, Inc.*
Chief Wagon Officer: Mr. Robert Pasin
By Ms. Amy Bastuga, Vice President of Human Resources

Responsible for overall leadership of the global Human Resources function and key culture architect.

Our Company

Robert Pasin, Chief Wagon Officer, heads Radio Flyer Inc., the business founded by his grandfather in 1917. Radio Flyer is an iconic brand that holds a special place in people's hearts because it instantly transports them to a happy time — to the best parts of childhood. Radio Flyer, maker of the famous and beloved Little Red Wagon and the world's leading producer of wagons, tricycles, pre-school scooters, and other ride-ons, has more than 100 award-winning products available in 25 countries. Since 1917, Radio Flyer has created icons of childhood, building a legacy of high quality, timeless and innovative toys that spark the imagination and inspire outdoor, active play and we continue our dedication to bringing smiles to children & families around the world and to create memories that last a lifetime.

__Our Vision:__ To be the world's most loved children's brand.

__Our Purpose and Why- Our Mission:__ To bring smiles to kids of all ages and to create warm memories that last a lifetime.

__Our Service Ideals:__ We follow the LITTLE RED RULE: "Every time we touch people's lives, they will feel great about Radio Flyer."

__Our Shared Values and Beliefs:__ We are committed to the FLYER code:

FUNomenel Customer Experiences
Live with Integrity
Yes I Can
Excellence in Everything
Responsible for Success

Our Dividends and Accolades/ROI

Named to the Inc. 5000 fastest growing companies list, Chicago Product Innovation award winner, #1 on 50 Best- America's small and medium companies to work named by Fortune 2015, #1 Best Places to work in IL 2015, and a history of being named to several other award winning workplaces lists including: Crain's Best Place to work in Chicago, 101 Best & Brightest and the Wall Street Journal- Top Small Workplaces.

Our perception of the greatest challenge facing businesses in the coming five years

Employee engagement has been the bedrock of our own success so we know its value. In the coming years, businesses the world over are going to be challenged like never before to maintain high levels of employee engagement as multi-generational workforces combine with increasing decentralization of traditional office locations. The shift to work-anywhere approaches, while, promoting greater flexibility and a decrease in real estate expenses for companies, will require even greater efforts to maintain employee engagement in order to best serve the customer, and the company as a whole.

ABOUT THE AUTHOR

Nicole Martin

CEO, HRBoost, LLC.

Nicole has been recognized by numerous organizations for her commitment to professional excellence and her community. These include the Daily Herald Business Ledger Influential Women in Business award, a Women of Distinction honoree and, most recently as a 2016 Enterprising  Women of the Year Champion by Enterprising Women Magazine. As a highly regarded and sought after expert, her knowledge and advice have been featured in newspapers and magazines throughout the country. She has been featured by Forbes.com, the Daily Herald Business Ledger and Fast Company.

A self-professed "country girl in disguise," Nicole Martin grew up in Montana. The small town setting, where everyone knows you and greets you on the street, was the foundation for her dedication to transparency and accountability in all ways, both personal and professional. Nicole was fortunate to have a great mentor early in life: her mom. A highly spiritual woman, Nicole's mother raised her with the philosophy of being joyful and living in gratitude. She ingrained in her the belief that every person is special and unique and that we are each capable of pursuing our passions.

Nicole Martin does her best to share her expertise, not just as a senior executive, but as a thought leader, public speaker, internet

Advisor.tv host, author, board member and volunteer. As an ambassador for *Best and Brightest Companies to Work For™*, she has helped Chicago businesses see all the benefits a fully integrated culture strategy can bring.

Nicole now leads as CEO of her own successful company. As a dynamic and empowering consultative leader and futurist, skilled in helping organizations meet their strategic objectives through their people.

Her expertise provides more to an organization than just a corporate culture boost or a good office vibe. She links **human capital** directly to profitability time and time again.

Nicole resides in a northern suburb of Chicago with her husband, Brian and their two sons, Jack and Joseph. To learn more *visit www. hrboost.com* or follow Nicole Martin on Twitter @HRBoostLLC.

REFERENCES

Chapter 1

[1] Asghar, Rob. Millennials are the True Generation. *Forbes.com*. Web 11 Nov. 2014.

[2] Pearce, Fred. The Coming Population Crash and Our Planet's Surprising Future. Boston: Beacon Press, 2010. Print

[3] Figure 1.1. The Central Intelligence Agency. The World Factbook sourced from Wikipedia.com/World Population/Global Demographics.

[4] Mutikani, Lucia. Record high U.S. job openings point to skills shortage. Reuters. Web 9 Sep. 2015.

[5] Meister, Jeanne, and Karie Willyerd. The 2020 WorkPlace. New York: HarperCollins, 2010. Print

[6] Sugars, Brad. How many jobs can your start-up create this year? Entrepreneur Magazine. Web 14 Jan. 2012.

[7] Moore, Steve. The Great Worker Shortage. Forbes.com. Web 31 Mar. 2015.

[8] Reinhardt, W.; Schmidt, B.; Sloep, P.; Drachsler, H. "Knowledge Worker Roles and Actions – Results of Two Empirical Studies." Knowledge and Process Management 2011.

[9] Womack, Chris. Minding the Gap: A Roadmap for Addressing the U.S. Manufacturing Skills Shortage. Web Q1 2015.

[10] Karsh, Brad and Courtney Templin. Manager 3.0 A Millennials Guide to Rewriting Rules to Management. 2013

[11] Shane, Scott. Are Millennials Really the Entrepreneurial Generation? Entrepreneur Magazine Web 4 Feb. 2014

[12] Taylor, Paul. The Next America: Boomers, Millennials, and the looming generational showdown. New York: Public Affairs. 2014.

13 Biag, Mehroz. Women in the Workforce: What Changes Have We Made? Web HuffPost Business. 2013

14 Stone, Paula. "OPTING OUT" Challenging Stereotypes and Creating Real Options for Women in the Professions. Research Symposium: Gender and Work Challenging Conventional Wisdom. Harvard Business School. 2013

15 Last, Jonathan V. What to Expect When No One's Expecting: America's Coming Demographic Disaster. New York: Encounter, 2013. Print

16 Opposing Viewpoints® The US Census. Farmington Hills: Greenhaven Press, 2012. Print

17 Schmid, John. Journal Sentinel. Manpower says skill shortage continues. Web. 18 May 2015.

Chapter 2

18 Katzenbach, John R. "2013 Culture & Change Management Survey." Survey. Booz & Company, 2013.

19 Hamel, Gary. What Matters Now: How to Win in a World of Relentless Change, Ferocious Competition, and Unstoppable Innovation. San Francisco, CA: Jossey-Bass, 2012. Print.

20 French, Wendell L., and Cecil H. Bell, Jr. Organization Development. Upper Saddle River, NJ: Prentice-Hall Inc., 1999. Print.

21 Lewin, Kurt. Field Theory in Science. New York: Harper: 1951, John Kotter, Leading Change. Boston: Harvard Business School Press, 1996.

22 Nadler, David, and Mark B. Nadler. Champions of Change: How CEOs and Their Companies Are Mastering the Skills of Radical Change. San Francisco: Jossey-Bass, 1998. Print.
    Hiatt, Jeffrey M., and Timothy M. Creasy. Change Management: The People Side of Business. Prosci Learning Center Publications; Second edition, 2012. Print.

23 Hiatt, Jeffrey M. ADKAR: A Model for Change in Business, Government and Community. Fort Collins, CO: Prosci, Inc., 2006. Print.

24 Sweet, Neesa. Personal Interview by Nicole Martin. 11 Nov. 2015

25 Cloud, Dr. Henry. Necessary Endings. New York, NY: HarperCollins, 2010. Print.

26 Norton, David P. Retaining Your Best People. Boston, MA: Harvard Business School, 2006. Print.

27 Wiete, Aubrey Krekeler. "Connecting Organizational Culture to Performance." HCI Research (2013). Print

28 Colker, Dr. Jay. Personal Interview by Nicole Martin. 18 Mar 2015

29 Jandt, Fred E. Intercultural Communication. Thousand Oaks, CA: SAGE Publications, 1998. Print.

30 Hyun, Jane, and Audrey S. Lee. Flex: The New Playbook for Managing across Differences. New York: HarperCollins, 2014. Print.

Chapter 3

31 ERE Media. "Is It HR's Role to Support the Company, Or Its Employees? *Talent Management and HR*. Web. 31 December 2015.

32 Ulrich, Dave. Human Resource Champions. Harvard Business School Press. Boston, Massachusetts. 2005. Print.

33 Gurchiek, Kathy. SHRM News about SHRM. "SHRM Goes Live to Address Trends, Challenges Facing HR" Web. 10 December 2015.

34 McIlvaine. Andrew R. HR Executive Online. The Competency Question. LPR Publications. Web. 12 January 2016.

35 Towers Watson,. "The Power of Three." Perspectives **Journal Info** (2015): Towers Watson. Web. 8 Jan 2016.

36 PwC Saratoga,. "Managing people in a changing world. Key trends in Human Capital." PwC Saratoga (2008): http://pwc.blogs.com/files/key-trends-in-human-capital.pdf. Web. 5 November 2013.

37 Amy Adkins. "Majority of U.S. Employees Not Engaged Despite Gains in 2014." Employee Engagement (2015): Gallup . Web. 15 Feb 2015.

38 Crossland, Justin. "Employee Wellbeing: taking engagement to the next level. " Perspectives Employee Engagement (2010): Towers Watson. Web. 11 Nov 2013.

Chapter 4

[39] Russell, Charles. About Assessments. Feb. 2015. Web. 8 Feb. 2016.

[40] Hamel, Gary. What Matters Now: How to Win in a World of Relentless Change, Ferocious Competition, and Unstoppable Innovation. San Francisco, CA: Jossey-Bass, 2012. Print.

[41] Russell, Chuck. Right Person, Right Job: Guess or Know: The Breakthrough Technologies of Performance Information. Atlanta: Johnson & James, 2003. Print.

[42] Goleman, Daniel. Emotional Intelligence. New York: Bantam, 1995. Print.

[43] Greenleaf, Robert K. "What Is Servant Leadership? - Greenleaf Center for Servant Leadership." Greenleaf Center for Servant Leadership. Mar. 2016. Web. 23 Mar. 2016.

[44] Albrecht, Karl, and Ron Zemke. Service America!: Doing Business in the New Economy. Homewood, IL: Dow Jones-Irwin, 1985. Print.

[45] Katzenbach, Jon R., and Douglas K. Smith. The Wisdom of Teams: Creating the High-performance Organization. Boston, MA: Harvard Business School, 1993. Print.

Chapter 5

[46] Yastrow, Steve. Brand Harmony: Achieving Dynamic Results by Orchestrating Your Customer's Total Experience. New York, NY: Tom Peters, 2003. Print

[47] Yastrow, Steve. Brand Harmony: Achieving Dynamic Results by Orchestrating Your Customer's Total Experience. New York, NY: Tom Peters, 2003. Print.

[48] Merriam-Webster. Merriam-Webster. Web. 22 Feb. 2016

[49] Bryant, Adam. Quick and Nimble: Lessons from Leading CEOs on How to Create a Culture of Innovation. Print.

[50] Stark, Peter B., and Jane S. Flaherty. The Only Leadership Book You'll Ever Need: How to Build Organizations Where Employees Love to Come to Work. Franklin Lakes, NJ: Career, 2010. Print.

51 Thompson, Kenneth R. It's My Company, Too!: How Entangled
    Companies Move Beyond Employee Engagement for Remarkable Results.
    Austin, TX: Greenleaf Book Group, 2013. Print.

52 Schein, Edgar H. Organizational Culture and Leadership. San Francisco:
    Jossey-Bass, 2004. Print.

53 "Guidestar, Inc. Clinical Dysfunctional Leadership." Personal interview.
    26 Feb. 2016

54 "Guidestar, Inc. Clinical Dysfunctional Leadership." Personal interview.
    26 Feb. 2016.

55 Goldman, Alan. Destructive Leaders and Dysfunctional Organizations.
    Edinburgh, Cambridge UK: Cambridge University Press, 2009. Print.

56 Fry, Dr. JP Pawliw-. "www.ihhp.com." Institute for Health and Human
    Potential , n.d. Web. 2.23.2016. <http://www.ihhp.com/dr-jp-pawliw-fry/>.

57 Fry, Dr. JP Pawliw-. "The Epidemic of Playing Small: The My Way Trap."
    SHRM National Conference. Chicago. May-June 2008. Lecture.

58 Bass, Bernard M., Ralph M. Stogdill, and Ralph M. Stogdill. Bass &
    Stogdill's Handbook of Leadership: Theory, Research, and Managerial
    Applications. New York: Free, 1990. Print.

Chapter 6

59 Porges, Stephen W. The Polyvagal Theory: Neurophysiological
    Foundations of Emotions, Attachment, Communication, and Self-
    regulation. New York: W.W. Norton, 2011. Print.

60 Hoque, Faisal. Everything Connects: How to Transform and Lead in the
    Age of Creativity, Innovation, and Sustainability. Print

61 Drucker, Peter F. The Practice of Management. New York: Harper & Row,
    1954. Print.

62 Benedetto, Ray Dr., and Steve Fallek. "GuideStar, Inc. Investor
    Prospectus: Appendix B." Mar. 2016.

63 Benedetto, Ray Dr., and Steve Fallek. "GuideStar, Inc. Investor
    Prospectus: Appendix A." Mar. 2016.

64 Benedetto, Ray Dr., and Steve Fallek. "GuideStar, Inc. Investor Prospectus: Appendix C." Mar. 2016.

65 Tabrizi, Behnam N., and Michael Terrell. *The Inside-out Effect: A Practical Guide to Transformational Leadership.* New York.: Evolve, 2013. Print

66 "What Is Appreciative Inquiry (AI)?" The Center for APPRECIATIVE INQUIRY Appreciative Inquiry. Web. 23 Mar. 2016.

Chapter 7

67 Wikipedia. Wikimedia Foundation. Web. 23 Mar. 2016.

68 "The Pinchot Perspective." 'The Pinchot Perspective' Gifford Pinchot III. Web. Mar. 2016.

69 Krueger, Allyson. "The Rise Of The Intrapreneur." Fast Company. 18 May 2015. Web. 23 Mar. 2016.

70 Benedetto, Ray Dr., and Steve Fallek. "Personal Journal: Character-based Capitalism Program." Module 3. 2016.

71 Collins, James C. Good to Great: Why Some Companies Make the Leap-- and Others Don't. New York, NY: HarperBusiness, 2001. Print.

72 Benedetto, Ray Dr., and Steve Fallek. "Personal Journal: Character-based Capitalism Program." Module 2. 2016

73 Towers Perrin Global Workforce Study. Rep. Towers Perrin, 2008. Print.

Chapter 8

74 Weite, Aubrey Krekeler. "Research - Human Capital Institute." The Human Capital Institute (HCI) and PS Culture Matters. How Building and Sustaining a Performance Culture Impacts Business Productivity and Financial Performance. Human Capital Institute, 2013. Web. 18 Apr. 2016